LATER

Also by Paul Lisicky

Lawnboy

Famous Builder

The Burning House

Unbuilt Projects

The Narrow Door: A Memoir of Friendship

LATER

MY LIFE AT THE EDGE
OF THE WORLD

PAUL LISICKY

GRAYWOLF PRESS

This publication is made possible, in part, by the voters of Minnesota through a Minnesota State Arts Board Operating Support grant, thanks to a legislative appropriation from the arts and cultural heritage fund. Significant support has also been provided by the National Endowment for the Arts, Target, the McKnight Foundation, the Lannan Foundation, the Amazon Literary Partnership, and other generous contributions from foundations, corporations, and individuals. To these organizations and individuals we offer our heartfelt thanks.

This is a memoir. Some names and identifying details have been changed to protect the privacy of individuals. Certain quotations have been reconstructed to the best of the author's ability.

Published by Graywolf Press
250 Third Avenue North, Suite 600
Minneapolis, Minnesota 55401

www.graywolfpress.org

Published in the United States of America

ISBN 978-1-64445-016-1

2 4 6 8 9 7 5 3 1
First Graywolf Printing, 2020

Library of Congress Control Number: 2019933480

Cover design: Kapo Ng

Cover art: Sam Chung @ A-Men Project (dog illustration)
Phase4Studios / Shutterstock (photograph)

For Polly Burnell and Elizabeth McCracken

The sand is the great enemy here. . . . The sand drifts like snow, and sometimes the lower story of a house is concealed by it, though it is kept off by a wall. . . . There was a school-house, just under the hill on which we sat, filled with sand up to the tops of the desks, and of course the master and scholars had fled.

HENRY DAVID THOREAU, 1865

*

The very houses are subject to change and move about as though not anchored to the land. In most places when a man builds a house he builds it and there it stands, practically unchanged. . . . This is not true in Provincetown. Houses there do not remain upon their foundations. Formerly, every summer one saw houses cumbrously moving down the front street.

MARY HEATON VORSE, Time and the Town:
A Provincetown Chronicle, 1942

*

This wasn't the sea of the inexorable horizon and smashing waves, not the sea of distance and violence, but the sea of the eternally leveling patience and wetness of water. Whether it comes to you in a storm or in a cup, it owns you—we are more water than dust. It is our origin and destination.

DENIS JOHNSON, Resuscitation of a Hanged Man, 1991

*

In Provincetown I was overwhelmed with this sky thing. It became a new character in my life and made me want to write poems. Then I realized there were skies everywhere, so that whole period of time I kind of made every poem I wrote touch the sky.

EILEEN MYLES, 1999

What happens to people out here on the Lower Cape, a mid-ocean sandspit, what happens even to intelligent and educated people, that they take to plying skies like cows in Chagall? From solid citizens they sublimed to limbless metaphysicians. Their minds grew lucent as gels. Or they slipped from super-saturation to superstition without passing through crystal.

ANNIE DILLARD, *The Maytrees*, 2007

*

Paul had begun to work out the taxonomy of Provincetown (should he say "P-town?"—he wasn't sure): performers seemed to occupy a stratum between tourists and townies—weekender tourist, all-season tourist, short-season worker, long-season worker, year-rounder worker, queer townie, fisherman townie—but which one he wasn't sure.

ANDREA LAWLOR, *Paul Takes the Form of a Mortal Girl*, 2017

LATER

1991–1994

1

Dream House

We're out on the driveway, my mother and I, leaning against my little red car. September 30. It's the first morning in months when it's possible to stand outside and not be wrecked by the heat. Fourteen hundred miles to go, twenty-one hours; a stop in Beaufort, South Carolina; another in White Marsh, Maryland. We'd known this day was coming since May 1, when the writing coordinator phoned to tell me I'd been offered the fellowship: a seven-month residency in Provincetown. We've had plenty of time to take in the good news, but the day of my departure still seems to come out of nowhere. It is bad timing, but isn't it always? The good news flattens us, as if we've both come down with the flu, passed it between us, on the coolest, driest morning since April.

My mother looks back at the house: the tile roof, the arched window, the date palm sprawling over the tight, pineapple-shaped trunk. The lawn glistens. Sprinkler heads relax after hissing out water. She is probably telling herself it's the house she'd always wanted, the house she'd invoked in a subversive challenge to my father: When you see me lying in the casket, do you want to say: I never bought her that house? So he bought the house, and to punish her, holds on to the New Jersey house, lives there alone amid a slop of bills, newspapers, and out-of-date engineering books, and comes down for a ten-day stretch only every six weeks.

She rubs her hands, arthritis twisting her forefinger, which she occasionally shows me just so she has a witness. I've been back only eight months since grad school, but it's also been a lifetime, as if I'd never left home and known what it is to have an adult life. She won't let me know how much she loves me, won't say how much she's going to miss having someone to talk to, but instead channels those feelings into lists, asking me if I've packed a razor, toothbrush, deodorant, contact lens solution, contact lens case, comb, dental floss, Q-tips, Band-Aids, blunt-tipped scissors: all the items so easy to pick up at a chain. She is driving me nuts, *knows* she is, but can't stop. Terrified of silence, she's lost her famous ability to laugh and listen. Not so long ago, on a trip to Morrison's Cafeteria, she talked incessantly for the full twenty-minute drive. I blew up and told her it was wrong to keep a running monologue, selfish not to leave any space for my response. Her face went red, as if I'd seen right into her liver and heart. She knew what I saw: someone who had lost her friends, someone who told them her secrets, and thus she withdrew, or they from her, as if direct talk about, say, her dead twin brother or her gay son named after him were too much for anybody to take.

I cannot be her husband. She must know I can't accompany her to Home Depot forever, pour shock into the hot tub, fertilize bougainvillea by the downspout. But does she say she can take care of herself on her own? That would be expecting too much. She puts her arms around me so I will feel the consequence in my body, the consequence of her losing once again. And I hug her back even harder in my attempt to do the impossible: push dark feelings out of her and leave light in their place.

Maybe she thinks, Why should he get all the freedom I don't have? Go to grad school, come back home, go off for a fellowship. Why should his happiness spring from, depend upon, my disappointment? What kind of logic is that?

Do you think I'm going to die, Mom? Is that why you're sad?

I want to say it, but don't. It would be cruel to go down those roads.

I suppose her heart wouldn't be so broken if I were headed to Arizona rather than Provincetown. Over the years our family has twice visited Provincetown, and we know what draws people there; we've walked among the queer people on the street, heard them laughing, carousing, seen the signals passed between them. She is afraid of my living among my kind, especially now that so many young men are dying of AIDS. She is expecting me to die of AIDS.

My mother. If I were studying my mother in a story, if I could step back from all my hot feelings, I could admit she still saw all the parts of me I've obliterated. The boy too anxious to eat his tiny sandwich on pumpernickel, the boy cowering before his teenage babysitter after she'd taken off his clothes. My mother must know I can be strong. And if she cannot help trying to beat some of that strength out of me, it's probably not just to keep me close, though that's part of it. She wants me to know that I can't lose my vigilance. She knows how easy it is to slip from one category to the next: health to illness, blind routine to misery. One minute she was a teenage girl working her finger into a hole in the floor, and the next minute, miles away, her father lifted his shotgun to his head and clicked.

I start the car, my eyes floody, burning. Tears drip off my chin, onto my shirt and shorts. It's quite possible she won't be all right. She isn't going to kill herself, I know that much. She isn't going to drink herself into a stupor. Nothing as extreme as all that, or even as rebellious. Her own killing will be softer. She doesn't believe in spectacular gestures, doesn't believe she deserves them. She does what people do all the time. Not making new friends, not allowing herself to be known, eating too much ice cream, no exercise, watching daytime talk shows that don't even capture her attention. Life as pure endurance instead of the hard, hard work of finding interests that refresh and nourish her.

She's been on another kind of suicide, but no one ever uses that word because it is continuous, cuts too close to home.

Who doesn't want to try to kill herself, at least once in her life, in a bad patch? You wouldn't be a human being if you didn't go there.

"I love you," she says.

"I love you too," I say. "Very much. And I think it's time we tell each other a joke."

"Joke?" she says, managing the impossible, tearing up while laughing.

"We're getting a little too serious, the both of us. Don't you think?"

And that stops her. The old pretty mother, the warm, dark-haired mother of the deep-red lipstick, flashes before me and goes. Who is this other mother in her place?

"I'm not as bad as I seem right now. I'm just exhausted. You must know that, don't you?"

"We'll be just fine."

"You promise?" She grimaces now. "You could sound a little more enthusiastic."

"I'll call you after I get to the motel."

"Don't forget, now!" she cries. As if I would ever forget.

I drive through pines and palmetto scrub, past lit signs taller than skyscrapers, a pink building in the shape of a huge sombrero, a dreamy wide river lined with moss-hung trees, the kind of river about which my father would say: I'd like to buy property there.

The kind of river you might choose to drown in if you found yourself in that frame of mind.

At a later point, I'll see my mother's rage as her strength. This refusal to regulate her sadness, this *no* to taming the inner animal of hurt. She must know this rage eats her alive, but that doesn't mean she doesn't want to soothe it, pet it, loosen its collar, and give it all the biscuits it needs. I deserved better, barks the glorious animal. I should have gotten more. And it runs around and around in circles looking for a way out of the fence, and it never gives up.

But I'm in no place to see that right now: I am all blind spots. I'm trying to be selfish, even though it feels like my left half is gradually being torn away. To steady myself, I conjure up a scene in which we're both undergoing surgery. Painkillers only when required.

2

Utopian

If you're lucky in your life, a place, or two, will be offered to you. That place won't be where you were born or grew up. It will be at some distance, and it will never be yours—you'll always be a visitor or guest. The trees will smell like rain. They might stay green all year, or their leaves might start browning in July as cool weather comes soon to these parts. Animals will be nearby, some of them in those trees, or right out in the open yard. The air will taste of ocean, negative ions churned up by the surf, or be so hazy your eyes will tear up and burn on sunny days—and you'll be fine with that.

This place will give you things denied you in your place of growing up. Company when you're in need of it, solitude when you're exhausted by careful, polite conversation without jokes. It will make you feel smarter than you are. It will make you younger, sturdier, more flexible in your joints and muscles. People treat each other better here, all of them, at all levels, and maybe there aren't even any levels, all the old ways we use to divide and rank one another. The lives of animals are important, too, not for human use but for themselves, in themselves, complex societies that care about their communities and want to stay alive as much as we do.

You love this place like a person you can't stop making love to— you dream about this person when they're right in front of you. You move through its streets and paths aroused and alert. You can't get that mischievous smile off your face. You want to put your hands on it, that place, that whole place. You have a secret, and isn't it lucky that everyone else on the street shares that secret with you?

Wanting

In pictures from that time it looks like my body and brain aren't speaking to each other. Certain parts ignore the other parts. And the ribs, lats, obliques, the shallow channel above the tailbone—they don't believe they matter. I expect clothes to do all the work of identity, as does practically everybody. In the era of AIDS, clothes are enormous. They function as armor, or drag. They bestow power, but also swallow up whoever pulls them over their heads. Maybe the greatest taboo involves drawing attention to the body, as so many are losing theirs, waking up to find their wrists thinner, chests marked with spots and scale. And yet my longing to stand out—through a pattern or a color—is so strong I can't help but get it wrong. Pent-up desire makes me a little nuts. It makes me porous, warps my perception. Weird words come out when I don't expect them to. Desire flushes me with shame, the kind of shame I want to rub out of my skin until it relaxes.

The real me is not here but in the future.

And yet I've done everything possible to prolong childhood and delay adulthood—or to make sure that that future doesn't happen. I've gone from grad school to grad school, slept with three guys before I was twenty-eight. And that's all about HIV? The fear of? Too simple.

"I didn't hold you enough when you were a baby," said my mother the evening before I left. We sat at the kitchen table, shucking corn into a brown shopping bag. Immediately she looked like she wanted to take it back, even though her face also said she was giving me a gift, an act of tenderness she tried to pass on but couldn't. For a second I felt it pour through me (*everything is explained*), but then the room felt warm, too warm. She'd given me power over her by letting out a deeper secret: She was afraid of me. Even when I was a ten-pound baby, my mother was afraid of me.

Camera

Years back, I memorized all the Fellows' names, but the names mean less to me now than the group photo in the old brochure. It's a scrappy bunch. Peacoats and scruff and chapped hands and muddy boots. They stand outside a shambly cedar-shake building officially known as the Fine Arts Work Center in Provincetown, some on steps, some on the landing. Each person looks on-the-way-to-important but not self-important: they're too confident and wry and full of possible humor. They don't look burdened by their pasts, maybe because they're making work out of those burdens. They're bound by something ineffable, the gut sense that they're transforming their lives, involved in a task that matters. And they have company while they're doing it.

They're a version of a family, too, though I doubt they even knew this about themselves until the photographer lifted the camera.

Legs press against legs, arms toss over shoulders.

And now I will be in the picture.

Circus

The car climbs the hill, and at the top, wild space opens up ahead. And there it is, rising out of the water like a question, an illusion across marsh and platinum lake. The Pilgrim Monument, a twenty-five-story replica of a tower in Siena. The curved coast of the harbor, shining. The spray of boxy white cottages along the beachfront. Fishing boats, sailboats, boats of all types pinned to the surface like thumbtacks. Up Route 6 I've been driving in deepest New England, charming and astringent. Or through a version of my childhood woods, thick with pitch pines. And from here it's a tree-shorn city, stranger because I haven't driven toward a city in hours, not since Fall River. Who would ever tell that it's all of three blocks wide, three miles long? A long, reclining anaconda of a place.

And maybe that's why every attempt to lay it out comes up short. Every representation stretches out into failure. The temptation is to paint it gold and deep green, because that's what it stirs up in me: safety, connection, expression. But Provincetown is neither warm nor cold, and it's never in-between. A simultaneity of masks, a place constantly shifting like the light and the dunes. What should I expect of a town built on dunes?

I make the left turn onto Conwell Street. I pull into the parking lot between two buildings, one long and relaxed, the other stubby. A barn with a blue circular plaque on the shingles. No one's around but for a young woman with hunched shoulders carrying pots and pans from her car to a doorway. I loiter in the car for a minute, head down, moistening my dry lips. Why is my pulse racing? Maybe she'll go away.

When she leaves, I walk into the office. Friendly, tight handshakes—Michael? Robert? I tell myself I cannot forget their names and then I instantly forget their names. The person in charge passes a key into a tiny manila envelope and offers me a handout of instructions.

I want them to think they've made the right choice by inviting me here. Maybe if I'm sweet enough, funny enough, they won't know that I'm a fraud, that it takes me hours to put the simplest paragraph together, that I distract myself from my work as soon as the writing goes well, and I'm too flustered to sit down at my desk for more than twenty minutes at a time.

I pop open the hatchback. Suitcase, duffel bag, boxes of manuscripts, floppy disks, envelopes of positive rejections, which I think of as my hall of shame. I trudge up the stairs, their thin carpeted treads. Running up and down, up and down. Somehow I manage to empty the hatchback in five minutes flat. I sit cross-legged on the floor of my long, narrow space, the second floor of a Cape Cod. One window to the north, the other to the south. Dormer in the living room. Strip of kitchen fixtures to one side. Narrow bedroom, single twin bed up against the wall. Enough room to fully stand up only within three feet of either side of the ceiling peak. A boxcar, a monk's space. A little disappointing, to be frank, with just a hint of Florida on the air. By Florida I mean mildew. Flat soaps and squat motel glasses trapped inside a waxed sleeve. Not the Florida of the present: my parents' house.

I lie on the bare mattress, fully dressed, look up at the ceiling. Something singes my eyebrows. Or is it just death grabbing at me, the voice of my mother pulling me down, down? Why has my father run away? I want something that isn't directly in front of me, which translates itself to desire. Desire is a condition I can manage.

Though the night is quiet (crickets, sitcom laughter from a wide-open window), I can't sit still. There is a town out there, a circus, and I have been dead too long.

Movie

It's October, and life is about to change for all forms: animals, humans, plants. Town seems less like the beach towns of my childhood, and behaves more like a metropolis. The harbor is secret, tough to find, the openings narrow and few. Smelly, weedy, industrial. No settler could have predicted tourism: who'd ever want to visit the windiest place on the East Coast, where loose sand once buried the houses to their eaves? It must have made sense to wall off the water, to shut down the view. For mariners and fishermen, the sea was work, the life they wanted to get away from. That sea could murder you too.

So the street means more than it does in other places by the sea. Commercial Street is as wide as a rural drive, constrained on either side by stores. It pretends it's a boardwalk but has no open horizon to calm frenetic minds. People don't disappear; people are larger here. Voices, faces, gestures, the cuts of jeans, shirt patterns. Clothes appear to be chosen experimentally, expect to be remembered, recorded. Commercial Street purring with the expectations of a catwalk, even when there's no one awake to spy, interpret, pass on what they've seen.

Haven

How far has my life been from my body, my breathing, my posture, my silliness, my joy? I stand up straighter, my shoulders fall backward as if they've been held up for too long by pulleys and strings. My walk changes, too, or so I imagine; my heels strike the pavement as if I'm possibly damaging my feet. This is what power feels like, but only when power is spread evenly, or when queerness isn't othered but is central. I look at people's faces; people look back at me, not exactly with need but curiosity: Who are you? And never the stench of judgment. No expressions that say ugly, weak, failure, get out, go back to your country, I'm going to rape you.

To be freed from the day-to-day expectation that someone's out to kill you. The air alive with released human energy.

But how will I ever be able to leave this haven, so far from the repression and punishments of adulthood? Am I trapped in sweetness now?

I've been given the cake of the afterlife and I can't help but taste the chemical on my tongue.

Mystery

From now on I'll call it Town. In that way I'll keep it a mystery, take it back from all my old associations, commercial, poetic, a visual artist's capital of light. Anything too sociological. Anything known. Town as much a *myth* of community as a place attached to the earth. Town embedding a notion of how to live with one another, even if it's falling short of its ideals, yes, failing on a daily basis, and still going on.

Town moves on two tracks at once. The time of narrative—in which people want things and lose things—and lyric time, which has nothing to do with the clock. It floats, and it isn't quite attached to Town but is part of its structure—what draws people here whether they realize it or not. Clock time moves forward but lyric time moves off to the side and stalls: lateral instead of linear. It's time as enacted in a painting or a poem or a song. It was around before humans and it will exist long after humans are gone.

The Grid

I've grown up thinking of the ocean as being in the east, so why is the water in the west? Town scrambling my coordinates once again. On a map, the Cape appears as an arm bent at the elbow, hand gone absolutely relaxed. Town situated on the final joint of the longest finger—the fuck-you finger—facing southeast. The center point of a spiral, a fury of wave and windstorm and sand. Who knows where I am now, and now, and now? Though I love music that shifts rhythms, tears up the harmonic structure, and changes key just as things get safe, I'm probably drawn to these qualities because I'm more attached to the grid than I know: a north–south directional attunement that lets me guess the time and temperature within a shade or two of the exact reading. But there's no grid here, at least not one aligned with the compass. West means as much as south. It's like living inside Joni Mitchell's "Hejira" in which the guitar is retuned to preposterous notes and I'm left to find the chordal shapes on my own.

More San Francisco than San Francisco

I keep walking until the lights go off in the houses, and there's no more street left to walk, just the bay bisected by a thin breakwater that reaches like an arm of a clock into the dark.

It isn't my first walk in Town but an early walk. I don't yet know that sex is never really just sex here. In a small town where everyone values privacy, I probably still have the hungry look of a tourist who's never going to be heard from again. Thus I am "talent," a designation that lasts all of a few days, until somebody figures out I'm not driving back over the Bourne Bridge anytime soon.

The tall blond guy stands in front of the head shop, one of the beating hearts of Town. It is bright with pink and green Day-Glo, obscene bumper stickers in the front window, and possibly monster dildos hanging from hooks in the ceiling. I usually don't take to blonds, but he has a rangy, goofy energy in the manner of a cartoon dog like Scooby-Doo. He doesn't present as queer, or even comport himself for others who might be queer: no military haircut or goatee or red bandanna on his head. His hair sticks up then falls down, as if he might comb it every three days, or whenever it occurs to him. His eyes are blue, unexpectedly kind. He's still a boy, though he might be twenty-eight. He has the look of someone who doesn't have a family, doesn't have a best friend, or any close friends, really, just a lot of noisy people swirling around him feeding him any powders and pills he wants.

"Hey, do you want to get high and have sex?" he asks.

And because I haven't touched anyone since God knows when, and because I'm possibly flattered to be chosen, I say yes to the cracked glee of this, the easiest yes I'll ever say about sex in my life.

But what do I want? Instantly it stops feeling so easy. As we're

15

walking up the stairs, I think, Why am I here? Can I back out now, run down the street? I want to lose myself a little while, I want to connect. I want to inhabit another plane that doesn't put the spoken front and center. I want to summon up the other times I've had sex, at least the good times I've had sex. I want to feel embarrassed, because to feel embarrassed is to feel broken open, alive. I want to read someone's sounds and reactions, second by second. Skin against warm skin, even if the bottoms of my feet are rough, cold. He must be nothing more than his dick, his arms, his ass, his scrawny white chest, his kiss.

Why should all of that be impossible?

But of course it will be impossible. A puzzle piece will fall onto the floor, get kicked under the rug. He'll tell me too much about himself; he'll tell me he likes hamburgers; he'll tell me he went to Catholic school, he wants a motorcycle, a cobalt-blue helmet—he won't stop talking. I won't be able to project onto him. Instead, I'll be running laps around my head, and not in my animal body.

My animal body—I want to bring that back too. The animal I came from before ancient people started thinking: *relationships.*

We're on the bed of a second-floor bedroom of a violet Victorian with dragons and gryphons in the side yard—more San Francisco than San Francisco. It is very dim, and I don't see any objects inside. No mementos or pictures of old boyfriends or siblings on the tall dresser. No shades or even a torn sheet over the windows. It's the room of someone who hasn't ever moved into his life, and probably never will. Why bother at this late hour?

He doesn't ask who I am or where I'm from, which is a relief. I take a long drag from the pipe he offers and choke back my cough. It seems very important that I follow his lead, if only because I want him to see that I don't want too much out of this. It certainly helps that I'm not attracted to him, and know exactly how I feel about him. I'll definitely not be pining for him anytime soon, and though that should help, it doesn't. Every few minutes a passing look in his eyes suggests he's scared of me, but maybe he's just mirroring the look I'm giving back to him. It's hard to know if I'm scared when I'm right on top of those feelings.

Is my dick still hard in spite of all my busy thoughts? Amazing.

What I'd give to be back home right now, wiping down the sink or putting the objects of my mess back into drawers.

I'm still watching him, watching myself from some safe distance when he pulls out a condom. Even though he's three times higher than a kite he pulls out a condom. He rolls it onto me, even if, in his case, he appears to be just taking me into his mouth. We're close to AIDS, so close it's almost inside before it's even inside. By that I mean the *idea* of it: the air we breathe is drenched in its possibility. And that's why it doesn't even occur to us to be bothered by latex, the smell and gummy barrier of it.

Wetsuit for deadly times.

Afterward, he dashes over to the bathroom sink and spits, as if he's been given a taste of raw blood. I tell myself it's good he's careful about health, even if his mouth never got near my skin.

But I'm a little annoyed too. That's *me* he spit into the sink, dammit.

Nights of Cabiria

On some nights the moon in Town is the moon from *The Tempest*, but with sex and menace in it; it sweeps down on the rooftops and harbor. There's no other place I'd rather be. It tells me I was foolish to expect anything less of the world than this—why am I always putting up with less? The harbor is a cup that was made for this moon. It holds and shimmers it, backlighting the shapes of the boats and the breakwater. The light doesn't move in a straight line. Instead it concentrates, shifting to the left and right like a river moving downstream. There's even an oily pool in the center of that light—water upon water. It's so strong it falls outside its corridor, throwing sparks that shock and dazzle the surface. Rather than a Shakespeare moon, it is a Fellini moon, transferred from film stock to everyday life.

It doesn't hold itself to the harbor, but saturates the houses too. I'm not here on earth anymore. Every street in Town leads to this light. It knocks whatever trail of thought I'd been following right out of my head. Maybe I can't even hold a conversation when this moon is nearby. Brenda Shaughnessy's moon: "You change shape and turn away, / letting night solve all night's problems alone."

Is this light a devil? If so, the devil has never been so pretty.

It works into my room, works into the cracks between the cabinets, underneath the rugs, until nothing is left unlit, untouched, uninfected. Nobody, nothing can hide from that moon.

Golden Gate

Maybe it's easier to leave the world when it's unstable, pitched on the end of a peninsula, indeterminate as the fog that rolls in over rooftops, dormers, houses on hills, forking through the oaks and hickories as if they're redwoods.

The Lamp

Commercial Street is dense with apartments and rooms impossible to ever fully know. Other towns live beneath the visible Town. I don't understand the conventional explanations of ghosts, but I do understand boxes of ashes stashed beneath drafting tables, the ugly shirts of the young dead still hanging in closets, the young dead crying, Now, get rid of them now—I don't want to be remembered by that tacky thing, too vivid and out-of-date. And meanwhile a man—I'll call him Tom—turns on a cheap little lamp, not suspecting the dead live in that lamp. The dead light up the room for an hour, while Tom drinks a beer gone flat, scratching his nose and watching the 6:30 news.

3

Star Boys

Fear of the Communion cup, fear of surgery: fear of contaminated blood, whether Christ's blood or your neighbor's. Life—blood, sexual fluids—is itself the bearer of contamination. These fluids are potentially lethal.

SUSAN SONTAG, *AIDS and Its Metaphors*

In 1991, 10,000,000 people live with HIV, more than 1,000,000 in the United States. In that year alone 20,454 die in the US.

Officially, there are 92 people living with full-blown AIDS in Town, which doesn't include HIV-positive people without symptoms. The number sounds low to me. There's no way to know how many people are positive in a village with a year-round population of 3,617. Is it a third? Half? Are half the queer men positive?

By the mid-1990s, it will be said that 385 people died of AIDS in Town. Ten percent of the population. Sometimes I say it back to myself aloud, in hopes that it will sear me: *ten percent*. And yet I can't *feel* statistics.

The dead by now include some household names: Keith Haring, Liberace, Perry Ellis, Rock Hudson, Steve Rubell, Brad Davis, Klaus Nomi, Ryan White, Amanda Blake—yes, Miss Kitty from *Gunsmoke*. But not everybody's famous like that. Every time I reach for a copy of *Manshots*, a porn magazine, on the top shelf at the Little Store, I don't even give the centerfold much more than a glance. Instead, I flip forward to the obituaries, which always fall on the final page. The obituaries are reliably thorough and affectionate in their meticulousness. They mean to do two things at once, to regularize the dead, with a particular emphasis on all-Americanness, and to elevate them to icons.

But what do the dead make of these accounts? Do they even care about purpose or meaning? Maybe purpose and meaning trouble only heady people like me—people not fully inside the present, too oriented toward the future. Maybe the star boys of porn want to be alive as much as it's possible to be alive, and that's their politics, their rebellion. Dreamtime, ecstasy, forgetfulness, proof that another life beyond repression is imaginable. They offer their bodies to be seen, taken, put to imaginative use. To serve as proxy. To be the rugged jawline you're kissing, the dick you're holding in your hand, whether it's imaginary or real. They teach us how to be men, how to position our seeing at the center of our lives.

At least the general public is getting over the dread of visiting a place known as queer. No more fears of catching AIDS from the servers. Gone the concerns about the lobster and lettuce on your plate. That was the '80s. Town then was a ghost town haunted not so much by the past as by the losses to come.

It's not so easy to seroconvert; most of us realize that by now, but that doesn't mean even reasonable people aren't still afraid and feel some duty to process those fears. Whenever I kiss a positive man in friendly greeting, I make sure he doesn't see me stiffen or hold back even a little, even though he'd probably read that as just another stance toward him. The truth is, he's probably quite used to it. He's ten times tougher than any of us think.

Me Llamo Go-Go

At the Work Center—we always call it that, rather than the official name—we are proud to be Fellows, all chosen with an eye toward inclusion and intersectionality, decades before the larger culture makes use of those terms. Luckily, after initial awkwardness, we enjoy one another's company. We've all been around enough to know that that is a rare trait in any group. What if we'd had to deal with pods, cliques, groups of people who didn't speak to other groups? It's a relief both to escape our categories and still retain membership in them: black, white, indigenous, queer, straight, Scottish, Israeli. Some nights, to stave off the off-season boredom, all those hours alone in our studios with our work, we hold impromptu dance parties in the common room that both parody and pay homage to the TV dance parties of the '70s (think *Soul Train*). We catch ourselves behaving like members of an extended family, one by one jumping up on a makeshift go-go box, or cheering one another on in a line dance. We're in the last moments of the era when wide numbers of people still dance, when they're willing to be expressive (or possibly ridiculous) in a communal space.

Do I miss home on nights like this? I have admit to myself I don't, which is new for me, secretly a relief and a thrill. My mother must hear it in my voice when she calls me on the phone. It must be a shock that I'm all right—or even better. I might as well be saying, I am having the best time of my life, without saying it directly, and if I am punishing her with joy, I am also suggesting she doesn't have to live the way she's living (fear, wariness of strangers, holding on, holding on), too blind to see the cruelty inherent in my lucky position.

It's not like she wouldn't have wanted to come along if she knew how to give up the things she loves, or the habits anchoring her there.

Roll Call (Fellows)

Tim, Marty, Helen, Nick, Jackie, Andy, Mary, Jordan, Alicia, Brian, Nancy, Dariusz, Deborah, Duane, Jim, Richard, Mary, Bob, Itty, Danella

Danella

Danella and I become good friends right away. Instantly she is my big sister, though she is black and I am white. Like me, she grew up in the Philadelphia area. Like me, she even lived for a time in Cherry Hill, and sometimes we are startled that we ended up here, in a place that resists the bourgeois comforts of our former homes and all their unspoken dedication to security and upward mobility. Her younger brother is gay and maybe our magnetic rapport feels like home to her. She calls us Laurel and Hard-On. We laugh a lot about the most juvenile things. We laugh until we've made ourselves almost sick from the laughter, which is its own kind of drug, though we don't do drugs, except for smoking the occasional joint she rolls. There is a fireplace along one wall, too large for the small, tight space, too grand. Light it, and the burning logs slam heat against the walls. It roasts everything in its patch, the arms of the sofa, the vases, the wood beams overhead, until it's all too hot to touch. My skin feels as if I'm on the way to getting a fever; my throat's scratchy, even if I'm sitting on the other side of the room, as far from the hearth as possible. I drink glass after glass of cold water. Danella puts on Inner City, Neneh Cherry, De La Soul, Soul II Soul, Queen Latifah, Naughty by Nature's "O.P.P.," "Optimistic," by the Sounds of Blackness. We spend a lot of time dancing in loose, awkward bursts—half-jokey, half-serious about it, talking with intense interest about the other Fellows or Georgie Woods and Sally Starr, the Philadelphia television personalities of our childhood, which couldn't possibly be of interest to anyone else within fifty miles. That's probably why we do it: to seal our bond. At the counter, Danella jams long carrots into a juicer, filling up its tub and collector with an orange almost too vivid to look at. Back in Philadelphia, Danella's brother has AIDS. He's been so close to death he could almost drink it.

Polly

Polly and I instantly become younger together—as soon as we meet there's no doubt she is my other new sibling. She is a painter in Town, her work drawing from elements of folk art to make her own constellation of images. Animals, performing animals, human hearts, doors, some of it tiny, *tiny*—all of it an indirect response to the crisis in Town, and outside, but never engineered. The work is wonderful in that it isn't willed. Though the two of us are capable of holding weighty conversations about depression, addiction, art, family, and relationships, we are also capable of cracking each other up. We meet one night at a party at Danella's place. She's pretty, vivacious, talky, someone who'd never hold back the naughty thing everyone in the group wants to say but won't. I love it when she laughs, her laughter reaching a high place as if she's singing. Then there is her regular spoken voice, tuneful too. I'm not surprised to find out she's a wonderful singer; she grew up in a family of singers. She instinctively harmonizes with any song playing in the room, a third above the melody, a descant. We entertain ourselves by planning an imaginary convocation called Yawehlu, a Town-wide event in which everyone sings the Catholic folk hymns from the late 1960s, accompanied by a hundred twelve-string guitars, led by a stylish nun with a face out of a Modigliani. But not before coming up with the names for possible theme nights at the A-House, the main gay bar in Town. One is "Creamed Corn," which we find hysterically disgusting, and neither of us feels the need to explain why.

The Bottom of the List

Within weeks I figure it out: everyday chores are harder here than elsewhere. To get a dimmer switch fixed. To make a copy of a 200-page manuscript. To get a new alternator for my car. To get the lock fixed on my PO box. It can take a whole week of my time, tracing my options, setting aside hours for the appointment when I finally get one. If I complain or ask the wrong question, my name goes to the bottom of the list, or is conveniently forgotten until I ask and ask, until I've made a pest of myself, and I feel resentful for not counting enough to be seen. After the job gets done I forget about the stress. Until there's a reason for it to start all over again.

White Noise

People's voices are louder in Town. They swell and boom and laugh in a way that is not just for the people in front of them but also for those outside that circle. Sometimes it's too much, and if I'm stressed, or worried about bills, I might even want to say, Knock it off! Occasionally the laughs are accompanied by hand claps, which sound like they might be about warding off skunks, which have the habit of wandering up the center of Commercial Street. Part of it is that there isn't a freeway nearby, no city-sized ventilation systems. The air makes a shape for those voices, holds on to them, the way it does cigarette smoke and other dangerous things.

Hungry

When I'm riding with my friends down Commercial Street—and it's inevitably my female friends, but sometimes my straight male friends too—I have the habit of growling quietly at the occasional sexy man whenever we're passing him in the car. In the aftermath I feel flushed, sheepish, possibly no more grown-up than Scooby-Doo from the head shop. It's a performance meant to make my friends laugh. It never accomplishes a whole hell of a lot, rarely even a smile or a look of annoyed curiosity from the intended recipient. But deep down the impulse is less about trying to attract anyone than it is about showing my friends I have a sexuality too. They've been allowed to have that, all their lives. They've been allowed to hold hands in their high school halls; they've been expected to bring boyfriends and girlfriends home to meet their parents. They know what it's like to see themselves in movies, books, and on TV in forms other than pornography or some well-meaning movie of the week, so instructional and tentative it's cringeworthy. They don't know what it means to hide, or understand how secrecy goes deep in your blood, so that secrecy and desire are a unit: you don't get one without getting the other. And HIV is a hungry ghost: it wants to take away our sexuality before our health.

Sometimes I catch my straight friends scrutinizing me as if there's something to learn in my reactions, and they need it to understand themselves. They're watching someone grow up when they've been grown-up for too long. I don't exactly mind letting them see that I'm a good ten years behind them, a hormonal teenager in adult skin. And I don't mind being a teacher, just as long as they remember they're not in control of the narrative.

Sun City

At this point Town is a haven for the sick. Well, not just the sick, but people about to be sick, people who haven't shown any sign of illness aside from their positive test result. I assume they're in Town out of choice. They make a vibrating metropolis of a beach town, with its social services, excellent state health insurance, and the AIDS Support Group, which is the fourth beating heart of Town (the Work Center, the Unitarian Universalist Meeting House, and the head shop being the other three). It's the East Village drifted north, or the South End drifted east. I assume people have left good jobs, cashing out life insurance policies, living off their credit cards, in order to spend their last years in a place of camaraderie, beauty, and lowered stress. Almost affordable rents (at least in winter). A retirement community. Say, Sun City, Arizona, but for young men in their twenties and thirties.

(Are there actually old people in Town? Yes, but they're nearly all straight, Portuguese American people. As for gay men: old gay men don't exist in these times. You're ancient and rare if you're forty. The gay component of Town is completely young, but the young people have the physical problems of their grandparents.)

But not everyone has chosen to be here. Lenny Alberts, the Town doctor, talks about men being disowned, pushed out of their homes, fired from their jobs after being diagnosed. They end up here, on a strip of land surrounded on three sides by water, because they have no other place to go. It could be that some of the people here hate ocean air, hate the stone quiet of the winter nights, hate the A-House with its buckle-y dance floor, more slope than flatland. They miss city museums, galleries. Noise and clamor, multiple languages, people of all colors, not just white people. A subway into a different part of the city, for example, Flushing or Sheepshead Bay, where they could go to a restaurant and eat a dish with a name they might struggle to pronounce.

Three-Way

I have never been around so many queers in one place before. Some would use that as a reason to stay single—why tether yourself to one person when you could spend successive nights with him and him and him and him? I, however, respond to this plethora of men the way I do when looking at the menu of a Greek diner: I point to the veggie burger, slam the menu shut, and push it across the table so I won't be psychically overloaded.

Which is another way of saying: I want a boyfriend.

I'm well aware that one of the reasons I want a boyfriend is to signify to others—particularly through the catwalk that is the main street of Town—that I'm lovable. A boyfriend is as much a public pact as a private one. And somehow I have gotten the notion that I need to be with someone else in order to be happy. It didn't start in Town, but someplace earlier where relationships were presumed to be a duty of growing up, like buying insurance or a first car. Maybe this comes from growing up near Philadelphia, where single people are usually looked at with caution and concern, and family life is all.

So what stance to take on? Or do we not choose our stance, and it is written in our childhoods, or in our DNA, long before we're in the world? Is a boyfriend someone to love, or someone to be loved by? All couples, straight or queer, position themselves along that fault line, though they rarely talk about it. I know how to do the first, but the second part makes me nervous, like an amateur. It silences me, actually. Dogs know how to be loved, but they are rare like that. For humans it's easier to turn one's eyes to someone else than it is to bear another's eyes on you. Those eyes come with expectation, wanting. Those eyes say, You might leave, so I will grasp on to you and do everything I can to make you feel.

As for the possibility of illness being a third party in a relationship? Well, imagine waking up one day with new sores on your back, tongue creamy with thrush. You can't even see your way to the bathroom. Your throat hurts. You've been feeling like your old self for weeks, staying up late, none of that dizziness when you get up from the chair, and now you're about to be in a bad patch, which might just be your final stretch. It's a big enough job to take care of yourself: it's already ten full-time jobs. How could you bear to catch the pain in your boyfriend's eyes, his desire to make things better? "*Fuck better*," you say aloud one day, just to test him, just to hear how it sounds in the air, and he weeps and stomps and tears a painting off the wall, all the while apologizing for his outburst. You want to tell him to go, but he's too lost in you to go. Is obligation murder? Too much to go wrong, too many feelings to be hurt. And the immune system—stress of any kind suppresses it. So the two of you tend politeness the way you tend the garden outside the window. The roses thrive, there's no scale or blight on the leaves, but your relationship? It doesn't die, though you never asked for a three-way with an illness.

Forty-Nine Degrees and Sunny with a Light Wind from the Southwest

I can't go to the post office or the A&P without running into someone with an appearance some call AIDSy—a little dark humor. He might be by himself, struggling harder than usual to get down the street with his cane. He might be twenty-nine years old. He might be in a group with others, whose apparent health only sets off his facial wasting, his sallow skin, his dry hair, which refuses to respond to any hot oil treatment. He's a skeleton with a layer of skin stretched over it. He might not have looked this way last month when he was doing dead lifts at the gym, so I make sure not to let shock show on my face. Or sympathy either—that would be degrading, condescending, a belief that there is a hierarchy of conditions, or simply two states: health and illness. I don't say, How are you? I never say that unless the person wants to talk about being sick, which is hardly ever the case. He'd rather talk about the weather, so I do, enthusiastically, perhaps too much so. I tell him all about the cold front and the possibility of tides three feet above normal by the end of the week. I say good-bye as if I'll see him tomorrow, locking his bike to the rack outside Town Hall, and I'm required to believe that as much for him as for myself. I must pretend that exchanges of this sort are absolutely routine, or I'll simply turn into a stressed-out mess, or become so numb that not a single sensation will pass through the membrane of me.

California, I'm Coming Home

> But we might wonder if AIDS, in addition to transforming gay
> men into infinitely fascinating taboos, has also made it *less dan-*
> *gerous* to look. For, our projects and our energies notwithstand-
> ing, others may think of themselves as watching us disappear.
>
> LEO BERSANI, *Homos*

My friend Nancy tells a story about Key West, a place she visits once a year. In some ways it's Provincetown's sibling, but its gay community is dissolving without being replenished. The living have had enough. They're cashing out or breaking their leases, settling north on South Beach or in Fort Lauderdale, where they're buying and renovating two-bedroom concrete-block homes once intended for retirees. When a certain server doesn't appear at the beginning of the tourist season, it's said that that person *went to California* as no one can stand to say one more person died. Have you seen Ray? Ray went to California. Where's Ivan? *Ivan?* California—he went to California. Richard, Steve, Jamal, Kenny, Toro, Juany—*they went to California.*

4

Paul

I wonder if my mother knew she was setting me up for trouble by naming me after her twin. Paul, who instantly dispersed into myth while she was left with none of the qualities you could put a name to. Paul, the perfected, the sweet, the funny, the gifted, the athletic, the effortlessly social—so rare no living human could ever measure up to him. To me, the name meant death, the one so good he was expected to be crushed and taken. I suppose my mother wanted to conjure him up by speaking his name once again. I suppose, too, she couldn't speak that name without putting me in danger somehow. Could she have cultivated that endangerment? It's always easier to love the departed one, the love purer, of a higher octane. It is an elixir when so much else is tasteless and weak, tea when it hasn't steeped long enough. Certainly she couldn't ever have said good-bye without imagining that being the last time, and certainly I must have done what I could to minimize the good-byes. Not just for her but for me too—who needed anxiety? Imagining a warm, calm bath filling around me, though I was always a nervous boy. To be nervous was to *be* her, or else to draw it out of her. I could be the dead one for a while.

She was afraid of my being the dead one.

The two of us were so close, death was all we could see in each other.

Vanishing Twin

When my mother is many months pregnant with my brother, an accident happens when she and my father are on their way to the lawyer to talk about her mother's will. They're in a nearby parking garage; water gushes down her legs as if it's vinegar, into her shoes, running down the ramp in a clear stream. Instantly they speed to the hospital—could it be possible to have a fourth miscarriage? My brother is delivered, but she knows that there is more *baby* inside her. She is convinced there is a twin in there, a dead twin, which Doctor Litz, her obstetrician, doesn't deny, but doesn't actually agree with either. Nevertheless, he describes for her the phenomenon of the vanishing twin, which dies to be absorbed into the uterus's walls. Sometimes that vanishing twin will be compressed into a flattened piece of parchment. She doesn't say if parchment comes out of her, but she knows, in spite of my brother's birth, that the story isn't finished. Story equals parchment. My mother will keep looking for twins, whether they're inside or out, and every possible twin, me included, is bound to hide, love, merge, separate, disappointing her.

Failure

Maybe my mother walks down her Florida street thinking others are saying, There's that woman, mother of a son she's ashamed of. What did she do wrong? And is that what it's like to live with head hung low, too lonesome to socialize with women her own age, who instantly pull out pictures of daughters-in-law and grandchildren, as if there's no other way to give each other value, currency. If she worries about that, maybe it's a way to stay close to *her* mother, who lost friends after her divorce trial got picked up by national newspapers. ("She could sell a dead horse to a mounted cop." My grandfather on my grandmother.) Funny in the context of the newspaper, but not when you have kids who can see it in print, hear it spoken. And a lot less funny after your husband's suicide. (Girl pointing to another girl outside the family house: "See that window? That's where the man who killed himself lived.") It makes sense that my mother craves boredom more than anyone else I know, to the point where it stops her from searching, from finding new interests. What's boredom but invisibility, power, the freedom to move among strangers without anyone making a target of you?

Isn't that what I want too?

5

New Boy

Every season there will be a New Boy—I've been told by a few acquaintances to keep an eye out for this phenomenon. He'll be absurdly handsome, with wavy dark hair and rugged features that set him apart from the prevalent look of white Boston. He'll have some mystery about him. A distinctive name, a movie star name, likely self-chosen the week before he got to Town. He'll often be within five years of twenty-seven, and will possess one feature of exaggerated musculature, say, triceps as wide as his neck, or heart-breaking lats. One year his name will be Storm, another year Echo. Once that boy becomes famous in Town, his name will come up at every party, every public event. To claim connection to the New Boy will be to confer prestige and value upon oneself. Have you seen Echo? Echo is looking for a new apartment. You have to see Echo's old apartment. He has the best view of the harbor. I think I saw Echo the other day? *Where?* Oh, Echo was at the A&P. Well, the next time you see Storm tell him Echo got a new haircut. Oh, what kind of haircut? A Caesar haircut. Oh my God, Echo's always so much ahead of the curve.

Will the New Boy enjoy his status? All those faces turned to him when he might once have been bullied or ignored? Of course he will enjoy the attention, but he will also feel the clock in his bones. If he knows his time is now, he will be smart enough to know someone else could sweep into Town and take his designation away. Invariably he will have one season. Invariably he will be trailed by that one season for the rest of his life, if he has a long life. Years later, someone will point to him, now a nice middle-aged man, and say, See that guy? He was once the handsomest guy in Town. And that statement will be delivered in a voice part sympathetic, part respectful, part laced with schadenfreude. And that man, should he hear that voice, will look forward and pull in his lips, carry himself as if those words had always been about someone else.

Mr. Mystery

As for me? I couldn't care less about the New Boy. He will never be for me; he's too much involved with himself. Not guys with classical features, not guys in powerful circles, or in any circles, really. Not even guys with *personality*, which can be collaged from movies and media and trash talk from the street. What do I want? Someone with the ability to turn the inner life outward. A stance that isn't always participatory. Warm, but a little cold, too, unreachable, elusive, removed. A quality that excludes me, that makes him feel that much more compelling—he's someone I want to get to the bottom of, even as I know that is as likely as a trip to the moon. He might play up something wrong about himself, a big nose, a jug ear, a broken front tooth, and turn it into the biggest gift of his life.

Factory

The hardest thing to convey: humans get used to this. They don't fold their arms with their heads hung low. They laugh, maybe they even laugh more than they did in better days. They live alongside this the way they live alongside all the earth's horrors: mass incarceration, racism, war, the memory or possibility of rape and harassment—where does the list stop? Sometimes there's rage, pus-filled rage, as livid as a blister, but not every second of the hour. People manage to get through the days, unless they find themselves at a memorial service.

Sometimes all it takes is an unexpected sign, a face or gesture conjured up by one word. And once that choking up happens it's almost impossible not to wail. It's almost impossible not to fall down.

Sleepy beach town: factory of death.

Several Feet Above

There were so many deaths that we didn't even know really whether someone had died or not. Somebody would say, "Oh, so and so died yesterday." And then I would say, "Well, I saw them at the A&P this morning." So Katina and I had [our] own way of de . . . of who was really dead, were they dead or were they dead dead? Dead dead meant that they were actually, truly dead. Dead meant somebody had told us they were dead, but we hadn't confirmed it yet. That's the way it was, so many people dying that you had to get to the dead dead level, then you would know there would be a memorial service coming soon.

JANICE WALK, *Safe Harbor/Provincetown History Project*

Billy's name comes up three times in two days. He isn't a writer himself but has strong connections to other writers, many of whom I'm getting closer to. All the enthusiasms passed along to me suggest that he and I would get along, either as very good friends or—something more? Oh, you'll love Billy. He's watched you walking down Pearl Street. He wants to meet you. Really? Me? Billy wants to meet me? Within a matter of days, Billy morphs into a kind of movie star in my imagination. I am excited about meeting this Billy. Billy is a smartass. Billy is from Lincroft, New Jersey, up the coast from where I spent childhood summers. Billy is an older version of the boys I grew up with, mean boys, snarling boys, boys I'd fantasized about, boys proud of their thick, arrogant dicks, boys who couldn't wait to take a shower in gym, calling me a fag for covering myself up with a towel the second I took off my pants in front of my locker.

I'm not terribly surprised that the actual Billy has nothing in common with this image. He is not tall, but not short either. He has a sweet face, is quick to laugh. His face is bewildered every time I talk to it, as if it isn't quite hearing or understanding every word, but thinks it's better to pretend it does. He is a deliberately ordinary guy, but maybe this ordinariness has been cultivated only in recent times. Maybe Town has cultivated it out of him.

If he looks like a movie star, he looks like Dustin Hoffman, but it's a younger version of Dustin Hoffman. Not Ratso Rizzo or the guy from *The Graduate*, but a lesser-known, quieter character.

One of Billy's projects involves photography. On his walls are his dreamy Polaroids, drenched in rich tones, resembling the dyes in food coloring. A navel orange, some open flowers, the shadow of an off-screen object suggesting a sprained plus sign. But the art closest to his heart appears to be cakes. His cakes are all over Town, from functions at the Art Association to AIDS Support Group dinners. Occasionally something is off about his cakes, though they are reportedly always delicious. Once, one multitiered cake collapsed when a knife touched its white icing. Another involved clear, water-filled tubes, and the goldfish that swam in them came to a tragic end in front of the guests of the party, who were expectedly devastated.

Billy looks at me with adoration, a special moon-eyed look like the look I'd get from a basset hound. When I look back at him with the special moon-eyed look of a basset hound, he looks back at me with confusion, as if I've misunderstood an equation as simple as one plus one. There's an endearing nervousness in his eyes, as if I am watching him take a pee by the road.

I'm supposed to be the adored one. It isn't the other way around, and when *I* try to adore I appear to take his power away, so I play.

He makes me dinner one night, but the dinner goes by so fast I'm not sure what I'm eating. We're pretending to be grown-ups when we have other things on our minds. All of a sudden Billy becomes romantic. He grabs me by the hand and leads me up the stairs to the bedroom, under a white steep-pitched roof, a bedroom inside the letter *A*. He starts unbuttoning my shirt, which always feels nice; I like to feel owned. It doesn't even matter whether I like it or not; I'm just relieved to be having sex again: a week is too long. Our clothes are off. The windows wide-open. The paperwhites and their foul smell, like a rotting bone. Fall air cooling our naked skin. Maybe just down the street someone is sitting on the edge of his bed, wondering when his coughs will go away.

"Billy?" someone says, weeks later, after I've let out we've been close. "You can do better than that." I feel bad for the character of the person who says that, but not for Billy. Billy will be all right.

There is lube, there is lotion. (I don't know why there is lotion here as anyone with any sense knows that lotion eats latex.) Condoms? I don't see a box on the table and I don't have one in my pocket. Billy's always been open about the fact that he's positive, so I don't know why he rolls over onto his stomach, and I don't know why I don't say, Hey, do you have a condom in the drawer? But anyone who's ever had sex knows that sex has a life all its own, and that's true if you're straight or queer. I want to make Billy happy. I'm afraid of confrontation, awkwardness. I'm watching two other bodies, several feet above the bodies we're in.

Two things are happening here: my desire to be above, my desire to be in. I must maintain both positions if I'm to get through this experience, the experience I want, but that I'm so afraid of.

I know the facts. I know it's unlikely anything lethal is running through my bloodstream right now.

And yet that shroud of, what? Guilt? Panic? I pull it around my shoulders, pull it tighter until I feel almost warm inside it. I should have watched out for myself, as if I were someone I actually cared about.

"OK, honey, I'm sleepy," Billy says, with sweetness, a boyish sweetness that masks the distance in it. "I'm sending you home now." He kisses me, dryly now, in the space where my two eyebrows almost meet. He sighs, part melancholy, part contented, as if he doesn't know how we ended up together in this era, in Town, not fifty years from now. As he doesn't intend to be mean, I don't receive it as mean. I walk up the street with five words in my head. One of those words is *boyfriend*.

Blood Brothers

My thoughts go to bleak places in the middle of the night, places they're not supposed to go. I think about the nineteenth century and Chopin, Keats, Emily Brontë. The romance of tuberculosis. The blood in the corners of the mouth. Bloody cough into the handkerchief. Little lamp on the table. The instant of transmission, voluptuous, fatal. We're all going to die anyway. Is it so wrong to want a boyfriend with HIV? I'd always be bound in blood, blood brothers. The same virus replicating, multiplying in our bodies in sync. If I were going to seroconvert—and if I had to—it would be preferable to get it from someone I loved. What could be worse than getting it from someone I wasn't even attracted to, someone I just had boring, rushed, and so-so sex with? *We're all going to die, anyway*, and I am tired of living on the outside. I worry about holding myself apart, a fear I've had all my life, some residue of my father's fear in me: distrust of others, their judgment. I want to be part of the story of my time, of my tribe. I'm afraid of never moving into my life, like the guy in his second-floor room around the corner from the head shop.

Maybe it's impossible to stop it, a wave that looks quieter than a tsunami. I put on my condoms. But blood seeps into a cut, a drop of semen creeps into a cut in the hand. One night I dream of waking up with a tingling in my hand, no feeling. Neuropathy. Or maybe I can't see out of the right eye, and I open the left even wider, *blink blink blink* in the hopes of blinking the darkness out. But if I were in love with someone, wouldn't company help me bear it?

One day a writer in Town reads a story in which the main character deliberately seeks out seroconversion. He wants to get it, with a pathological intensity, wants to give it out. Much later there is an informal name—bug chasers—given to such people, but not yet, and maybe that is why the audience sits through the reading transfixed, galvanized, scared, stricken. The story is too charged for people to talk about. Perhaps it's too much honesty, perhaps a telling detail or two makes more than one person mad: it pokes at too many taboos. And when the writer finally publishes the story, that aspect is picked clean from the narrative and only the bleached bones of its skeleton remain.

Head

It is said that if you buy a sex toy in the head shop, you must buy it from the guy in the back. Fried from so many drugs, he comments on your purchase, laughs at it, says something creepy, invasive. His brushy mustache, his leather motorcycle vest, his exposed sunlamped belly, which he displays, as if he's carrying twins inside him. He doesn't even like queer people—or any people for that matter. Drugs have probably blasted his brain clean. But maybe some want to be stirred up and tossed around by this person-hating daddy, so when they take their clothes off, they know how precious their purchase is. They know what it cost them, and thus how dirty they are, which has its imaginative uses.

Queer

> People can tolerate two homosexuals they see leaving together, but if the next day they're smiling, holding hands and tenderly embracing one another, then they can't be forgiven. It is not the departure for pleasure that is intolerable, it is waking up happy.
>
> MICHEL FOUCAULT, "The Gay Daddy"

The Provincetown of Freedom up against the Provincetown of Restraint: it doesn't take long to figure out that both straight and queer people fall on either side of the line. After all, Provincetown is geographically situated in Puritan New England, and restraint keeps buildings, yards, outfits, clotheslines, manners of speech in check. Restraint, of course, requires its opposite. Restraint tries to discipline and correct every time it encounters what it perceives as chaos, a threat to the social order: a dildo and harness in the window of the sex shop, blow jobs in the dunes of Herring Cove. It fears that Provincetown is continually on the verge of becoming a sex farm, a place in which children could possibly run into un-mentionable couplings on the way to the playground. Brakes need to be applied, if it's even possible to apply brakes to a farm.

And though it's less often said, the transgressor needs the Puritan. How could a gesture even be experienced as transgressive if there weren't the possibility of someone with folded arms, a hard, in-dignant face? Some from outside mistakenly think *anything goes* here, but they have no clue how necessary they are to the leather-man who walks down the street in a harness and high heels. The heels attack the pavement as if they're saying, Fuck you fuck you fuck you fuck you fuck you, even though the guy who wears them has the friendliest grin.

Gut Feeling

Confusion may be the only reasonable response to the world at present. And creating confusion may be queer's most useful weapon. Queer has no fixed fan base. Genders, races, classes: bring them on. But it has one broad political mandate: to foster instability as resistance to any status quo. Resistance is good exercise. It helps keep you young. And it can keep you alert. Even when you lose track of what "normal" is, you know you don't want to be that.

HOLLAND COTTER, "When It Comes to Gender,
Let Confusion Reign"

A stab of ugly deep feeling: I am here, in the place I've longed for, and community still won't come to me. It still won't close up the space. Town is distant, even though it's feet away from me. Four drunk women walk toward me, bump into one another, as if the whole point of their togetherness is to remind themselves that they have bodies, bodies that can be ground down, judged, dismissed. They want to transmit that gut, electric feeling into anyone in their vicinity. They're laughing, but it is a laughter that has much more to do with menace than joy. You don't have to live like this, I want to say, but maybe that's too simple. And I walk faster, eyes fixed on a store window, red hooded sweatshirts I couldn't possibly want or wear. I don't want them to notice me, don't want to be part of their continuous self-murder, the tricks they play to feel less alone. In Town, if they wanted to, they could become the bullies who once bullied them back home.

6

Uncharted

Provincetown wouldn't be nearly so compelling if Race Point weren't out there, if the Beech Forest weren't out there, if the fire road to the Hatches Harbor dike weren't out there. If the entire landscape was as *built* as the center of Town—houses all of a few feet apart, windows facing into other windows, fire hazard, really—I wouldn't have as much interest in it. It's good to remind myself of the uncharted forest, dunes, and marshes a half mile from the stores and bars. Late at night, if Town is quiet, I hear coyotes and foxes calling to each other. Sometimes even thirty-ton humpbacks, groaning and explosive as they shove water up through their blowholes.

Six Dogs

Billy wakes up to the sound of wailing one night. The wailing is ancient; it makes his hairs stand on end. It's 3 a.m, and outside Billy's window Anthony, an elderly, straight bachelor who grew up in Town, lifts the body of Charlie, his dog, into a wheelbarrow. He wraps him in a sheet. Kisses the top of his head, his flanks. Rolls the wheelbarrow forward, still weeping, but quieter, more controlled now, past his house, where shrubs grow through holes in the floor. Rolls Charlie's body to the dunes, a two-mile walk along the shoulder of Route 6. Is Anthony even aware of all the lost young men who have died in the last few years? Possibly not, but the rituals of burial are as familiar as oatmeal. Once he catches his breath, he starts digging the hole. Buries Charlie in the vicinity of all six dogs of his life. He sits there with his palm atop the sand until the sun comes up, when he has just enough strength to push the empty wheelbarrow back home. He would have buried Charlie during the day if burying dogs wasn't illegal.

Mountains & Canyons

It is a cold rolled across the sea, a cold pushed up from its bottom, which rises 194 feet (think a twenty-story building) immediately off Race Point. Mountain ranges and canyons hide beneath the surface, and the whales keep that secret to themselves.

I Saw the Plane

A small airplane, a two-seater, flies too low over Town one day, violating aviation rules. It crashes in the campground, killing the pilot, who is said to have been drinking, and his passenger, a woman he'd just proposed to at the Lobster Pot. It goes down in the weeds next to some tourists playing cards. Is there a single living being who didn't see the plane? "I saw the plane," says a woman who drives the Town trolley through the tight chute of Commercial Street. "I saw the plane," says a man buying gin at Yardarm Liquors. "I saw the plane," says a waiter, in treatment at Boston's Beth Israel Hospital at the hour of the crash, but who insists he's seen it with all the fervor of a Bernadette at Lourdes. Soon, it's not enough to have seen it. You talked to the pilot in your kite shop, served the fiancée oysters in your restaurant, drove the two of them in a cab somewhere and they looked edgy and nervous. These reports continue for the remainder of the season, into the next. You're not quite a member of Town unless you've had some congress with the plane.

Ptown

The name *Ptown* will never come out of my mouth, even though some I love will always call it that. Maybe it tends toward the slick. Maybe it edits out the unruly (that extra syllable), refuses to see anything beyond the party and the myth. Isn't that what Ptown suggests, Party town? But I love the party up against the struggles and failures behind shut doors, all the aspects of a place that can't be categorized, monetized, branded, sold, known. Leave Ptown— *I'm sorry*—to the people who call San Francisco Frisco. Who've left their hearts out there.

Mary Oliver

"Provincetown is the closest I have ever been to being a member of a society, a person in a community of people."

Myth

To live in Town is not so much to live in other places, where you're usually so inside the place you can't even see it. To live in Town is to explain it to others in an ongoing, continuous way that involves standing outside it—even if you're walking down its streets.

7

Canines

> There are many smiles involved in cruising. First comes the
> smile across the room, or across the street. This smile is the
> drop of fishing-line, a letter addressed to whomever receives
> it. The first smile communicates the cruiser's interest and
> availability; ideally, this smile meets with a smile that commu-
> nicates a specular interest on the part of the other. If smile no. 1
> is not met by smile no. 2, smile no. 1 may as well not have oc-
> curred. It is a tree falling in a forest without [an] audience.
>
> MICHAEL SNEDIKER, *Queer Optimism: Lyric Personhood*
> *and Other Felicitous Persuasions*

The man I'll call Philippe works in a gallery with an uncharacter-
istically flat roof and windows on three sides. He is skinny, slightly
younger than I am, maybe twenty-eight, with golden-brown curls,
high cheekbones, blue eyes. There is a crackle of sexual energy about
him, an intensity that would suggest he wouldn't know how to be
bored. He has the demeanor of someone who just discovered sex and
is tremendously excited by it, versus that of someone who's weary of
all its calculations—sex had gotten that other person into trouble,
but not Philippe. Philippe smiles at me one day, from across Bradford
Street, as we're walking in opposite directions, he toward L&A
Market, I toward the Work Center. I smile back. He is handsome
enough to be one of those people who always looks past and over
you, but he chooses not to, and I like that. How could I not?

In more ways than one he resembles an iconic figure in a porn
film, riding around on a tractor, with a hay stalk between his teeth,
pointing it up, pointing it down, pretending to play the role of a
Hollywood leading man on a pig ranch.

I see him around Town a lot after that smile. Now that the
weather's turned colder, he wears a battered black motorcycle
jacket, which appears to be his signature. Everyone in Town seems

to look like an actor, which makes sense when personality, rather than how much money you make, is the true currency. In his case he looks like a combination of Paul Newman (but younger, more awkward) and Starsky of *Starsky and Hutch* (but lighter, and less Jewish). His curls are at least a dozen years out of fashion, but he wears them as if he's confident of the gift they are—neither retro nor stuck in another time. Those curls and those eyes: the blue eyes especially suggest some woundedness, some danger, a need to test a threshold.

One day we end up on my twin bed, which feels like being back in high school. It's very easy between us, the erotic equivalent of tossing a football back and forth if I knew the first thing about how to toss a football. Or better: maybe we are two canines in the dog park, no human supervisors looking on. Mouth goes to mouth, hand goes to face, hand down to zipper, grabbing and holding on. He's wearing long johns. I rub his hard, fat dick through the front of his long johns. A guttural, secret parody of an evil laugh that is certainly not a polite laugh. I don't know whose pants go off first. Because we're approaching each other with equal intensity, neither of us is cautious or thinks, This is weird. We have the kind of sex that doesn't really ask much of us, and thus it doesn't really haunt or cut too deep. It isn't a transaction involving power. No one is expected to be the boss of it.

He plunks my electronic keyboard afterward, fully dressed now, no shower for either of us, and that is just fine: I like having his grassy scent on me. There is something endearing about the bangy, unsubtle sounds of his playing. He talks about wanting to come back, and I say, "Of course." Am I already thinking of him as someone I'd like to have sex with again? Maybe because the cloud of *boyfriend*, and all the social expectations pressuring that word, doesn't trouble the sky. He feels like someone I've known all the way back to high school.

"You shouldn't have sex with him," Billy says several days later when I casually ask him if he knows the guy, if he's ever heard of him. He says it in the voice of an old-school cop who's seen far too many criminals in Town.

I must look flustered, stupid, a little out of my element.

Billy tells me Philippe has AIDS. And has been very sick in the past, though you'd never know it now.

"But he looks just fine."

And Billy gives me an exasperated look, as if he shouldn't need to remind me you can certainly look just fine.

The moment swells. The clock slows as if it's dragging through maple syrup. I am weary that Philippe is just one more case—how expected. (*Fuck* it.) It doesn't even feel like a shock anymore. I am weary that I can't have the simplest sex without being troubled by questions—did I slip? was it risky to do *that thing*?—even when I've engaged in what's known as safe sex. And I'm unexpectedly melancholy that Billy would turn in Philippe, as if Philippe is part of some secret criminal gang out to expand its ranks. Such behavior would be condemned by other people with AIDS—Billy knows that very well. But I do not have enough distance to see that Billy is doing to Philippe what others have probably done to Billy again and again.

People take care of each other, and they don't. Both at the same time.

"Just watch him," Billy says, quieter, with less force now. Is he just jealous? One former New Boy of Town shrugging away another former New Boy of Town?

But Billy has shrugged me away every time I've looked at him with too much fondness, or stood too close to him at a Work Center function while others look on. I've given up.

Just the way I've given up on Philippe before anything had the chance to develop between us. When I see him from across Bradford Street, I wave, keep walking onward with a brisk and practiced grin. He doesn't look hurt, even though his posture suggests he'd been hoping I'd stop to say hello. If he's hurt, he's learned to hide it well. He knows better than to expect too much of anyone. We all do, sooner or later.

Refugee

Everyone has a designation, everyone is a story. Everyone is seen through the prism of his friends, whether he's a painter, a carpenter, a fisherman, a drinker, a pastry chef, a real estate agent, a person who grew up in Town or in California. Classes mix; people who have trust funds hide it, and are never caught wearing even a shirt with a collar. That would be the grossest display of indulgence in the last hours of bohemia.

Mostly people work themselves to exhaustion during the four months of summer, and for the rest of the year scrape by, getting through the winter on unemployment or on checks from Medicaid. They might have degrees from Harvard or Yale, or, if closeted, they might have climbed the ranks of the professional world, but they're never wearing that information on a placard. AIDS takes hold of a life, with all of its ideals and aspirations, and throws it to the pavement like a jar.

"He's positive," people say, not with judgment or unkindness, but as if that man were a refugee and he's never going to see his people again.

Pilgrim

I'll never forget in 1986, our first fall/winter, going to look at a winter rental, which was a guesthouse. It was during leather week. Entre Nous, it was called. The men were around when [Richard and I] arrived and one was ravaged. Gaunt, KS scars, hollow eyes. He didn't know us, but he said, "Look at me! I used to be a model . . ." and the other men were saying, "Yes—look—we don't know what to do. This is happening to us." I have never forgotten it. His leather jacket hanging on him, still handsome, David Bowie–ish. And how candid these men were, it seemed like they needed the witnesses, this young straight couple from another world.

POLLY BURNELL, on moving to Provincetown in 1986

On November 11, 1620, the Pilgrims entered Provincetown Harbor, where they anchored for two weeks after a rough crossing. Today there is evidence of them everywhere, in the names of the streets (Standish, Alden, Bradford, Brewster, Howland, Allerton) and in the Mayflower, the busy restaurant. Town could have made their narrative the centerpiece of its identity, but I wonder whether a few figured out that the brute side of the Pilgrims was at odds with compassion and cosmopolitanism. It wasn't enough that the Pilgrims were fleeing repression and regulations, in the manner of artists or queer people. Facts: Robbing the graves of the Wampanoag. Thieving their winter provisions, their stash of corn and beans. Not to mention stealing their land, pressuring some to convert, sending others away into slavery, even though they'd once welcomed and befriended the Pilgrims.

So Town leaves that first-landing designation to Plymouth, with its porticoed Rock, one hour across the bay. Town marks their arrival with an ornate monument that appears to have little to do with this history.

Frankly

You can spend the whole evening with someone. You can have the best time, you can say frankly sexual things, but with a laugh, of course, just to send a signal that you know talk like that is trashy. You can hold hands with someone in the backseat of a car. You can rub the knuckle of his thumb as he rubs yours, relieved that the sex between you, once you're out of the car, is going to be so easy and right. And just when it seems you couldn't be better matched, one of you will say, It was lovely to meet you, in a tone that attempts to mask that you'll never be anything more. If the tone were given words it would be something like this: I can't do this. There's too much feeling here, and I'll get pulled under by this feeling. My life will change too much. I'll lose my compass, my purpose. I've worked too hard for my freedom, too hard for my life, and I don't even care if I end up terribly, terribly alone.

A Thousand Little Grenades

Imagine it. Look at a drop of your blood, your semen, your saliva, and think of it containing a thousand little grenades. Not just for you, but for the lover you came into contact with. How would your life change? Could you disappear into yourself, into your skin, ever again?

Sorrow

Billy and I are driving back from Orleans, after an afternoon spent at the supermarkets and the single big-box store. We've enjoyed spending some hours together, clumping together to talk about a new cereal, then breaking apart to go our separate directions. Breaking apart, coming back together; it felt good that way. These trusting repetitions, like swimming laps at the pool of the Provincetown Inn. And just as we go over the hill by the Outer Reach Resort, Town comes into view, the monument, the marsh, the lake, the surface of which is wavier than usual: slate tinged with magenta. "It's beautiful," I say, and there's a sorrow in my voice, whose origins I can't explain.

And Billy looks at me, not glancingly, but stopping his face on mine, to let me know he means it. "It's so good to have your energy here," he says quietly.

My face must fall—or is it a twitch? Maybe I'm just thinking he's rubbing out the cloth, flattening all my creases. He's seeing only Billy, not me.

And then I open up again. A single emotion, like being dropped into the lake up ahead, but in summertime. Water as warm as a bath, salty and granular and full of health. For just a minute.

X

Emotionally it's a full-time job to draw a border between myself and my family, to decide I'm going to reject their unstated rules, their wishes for me. Frankly, I think some structural upheaval would be healthy for all. The unspoken dynamic in my family is that there are two choices—independence and interdependence—and the former is always a threat, without there being any middle space. Can't they see it? Do they want to? I'm positive they don't, and even though I can see it, that doesn't mean I'm not consumed with guilt, a quality I associated with a weak intellect in the past. That guilt is experienced as a sadness so out of sight it causes distraction, an inability to focus on my work, and leaves me with a need for sex as medicine.

Maybe my perceived withdrawal is strengthening the ties between them—now that I've given everybody a project, something to bond over. But I shouldn't so readily be offering myself up for sacrifice, or permitting it. We've been caught up in the currents of ancient Catholic ways, even though I grew up in a parish with felt banners, no kneelers, in a half-circular church that conjured up a jazz club. But the surface innovations appeared not to sweep deeper structures away, structures part of some oceanic past in thrall to— what? Secrecy, keeping power over people by naming a *few* prohibitions but mostly by not naming others. Prohibition: just about anything could fit inside the shape of its X if you allowed it to.

And maybe that's why my mother makes so much of sex, male sex, though she'd never admit to that. Male sex is uncontrollable, male sex is animal, it opposes us, oppresses us, it's what ruins the world and that's why we love it, why we hunger for it so, like we hunger for a father, even a nasty one. It is like nectar, it is our heroin. Milky and rich, filled with the protein and keratin of horns. All the ugliness in the world but within those drops the possibility of care, worth, affection, attention, and every value we can't name.

And if male sex ran out, there were plenty of other subjects, objects, rituals to fill the old need for withholding. The shape could constantly shift, the value could keep changing. Its purpose was to make all the rules around it impossible, inscrutable. It kept us on our feet. It sent effervescence, if already a little flat, into our veins. In that way the withheld was a little like God.

Cynical Workbook

A friend asks me how the prospect of illness changes people's experience of identity and time. What does it do to them? I am too close to the question to answer it. I am irritated with my friend for asking it, as if a question so big could be answered succinctly, just as I am irritated with myself for not being articulate, for giving him an opportunity to fill in the hole, which is just a poorly imagined narrative that might come from some cynical workbook. The cynical workbook says that people are preternaturally fucked-up, prone to poisoning themselves and others. The cynical workbook is nourished on the worst clichés of death metal and cyber intelligence. The cynical workbook is above all dismissive of human affection and comfort and the writings of Walt Whitman as if they bathe in a product called Sentimentality.

Maybe the better answer is this: If you are prone to awkwardness, illness might make you more awkward. If you are prone to craziness, it might just make you crazier.

8

Husband

After my reading at the Work Center, I meet somebody I've been seeing a lot of around Town. He has presence in his face, an alert and active expression. He's always looking, whether it's at people or houses or at the harbor, at low tide, at the end of the street. His eyes are so bright it looks like you could see all the way down into the clear, cold water of him. He is tall, a bit taller than I am, but not taller than Philippe, whom I rarely run into on the street anymore. He is relatively skinny, but carries himself in a way that suggests he wasn't always skinny; he knows what it's like to be thicker around the middle. He is a poet. His name is Mark. He speaks about my work like someone who knows his approval matters, and I am in awe, so grateful, my forehead moist with raised temperature.

Beside him is a woman who echoes some of his body language, though not like a wife or girlfriend. She walks with a cane, a stoop in the right shoulder. Has she been in an accident? She might be sixty-eight, or thirty-eight. In that way she has taken herself out of clock time, and it's no surprise to find out she is a poet too: Lynda. Black beaded dress, turban on her head, a cloche. Feathers? People dress up in Town, but she dresses as if she's in the city, not New York, but Brighton or Prague, in a basement piano bar where the people are too drunk to be jovial. Her outfit is in response to a world in which no one is looking, but we're looking. Some might say she is a female drag queen, but her style is more idiosyncratic and complicated than that, as she's not exactly making outsize statements about gender, nor appropriating another era and putting quotation marks around it. She is making something up about discarded things. She is constructing her own vocabulary of beauty. Her look wouldn't work for everyone, especially for someone who believes that fashion must be in dialogue with trends, but that's beside the point, which is that it's far from the standards she grew up with.

"That's my new husband," I say to my friends. We are walking down Pearl Street, in the dark, trailing the two poets, who are deep in conversation, walking close enough to be one person. I say it in a loud whisper, as if I half want to be heard by the people ahead of me, and half want to make my friends laugh at the dog of me: it's the verbal equivalent of wagging my tail. I'm developing a character of myself by this point. I am someone in a comic French film, or Buster Keaton, and it's a relief to slip into this other creature when I'm inarticulate, and nervous, and humor is the only thing to make the awkwardness of life almost bearable.

Plus, I'm a little giddy after having just given my reading. I think it went well.

"He already has a husband," Polly says.

"Of course he has a husband," I say, and the voice that comes out of my mouth is new to me. It isn't embittered or jaded. I'm happy for him. He glows. There is no question that someone like him, a human who looks at everything so he can transform it into description, has a husband.

Break Me

On the steps of the shoe store sits a man in a leather jacket, stubble on his face, pointy sideburns. He is in a mustard-colored T-shirt, scuffed black Doc Marten boots, with a red paisley bandanna on his head. He looks at me as if he's seen me before—at the gym? He has a style about him, the look of someone who's spent more time out in the world than on Commercial Street. Maybe Europe—his face looks very European, maybe Eastern. Or Berlin. Someplace where there's been an actual war on its soil. There's some shadow in his eyes, shadow beneath them. He is probably sadder than he knows. He looks seasoned, though I doubt he's five years older than I am. He has the demeanor of a person who gets some of his power from not looking at other people, so the directness of the gaze disarms. It has a weight in it, as if it expects a reply, and not just a hi. It says, You've been chosen. And I look off to the side—or down.

Small talk. I let him lead as I'm hardly ever the one to initiate. It turns out he knows my friends Jim and Jane, but I don't think he wants to talk about them, which might be why my reply is not terribly animated or inspired. I sound bored to myself, but I am not bored. By any means.

Immediately it's clear that Hollis is one of those people who make fun of you if they like you. If he doesn't like you he'd probably dismiss you, look right past you. It feels like a prize to be made fun of by him: he doesn't just give it away. He laughs, I laugh. He is obviously glad I laugh back, though there is a sadness and shock in his left eye that comes short in its attempt to conceal hurt. It's a stark hurt, and it's complicated by the sense that he has layers that probably can't be known. But he also seems to know just how he feels, and when he feels he transmutes it into a joke, with hardness in it. Any intense feeling is transmuted into a joke, the tactic a way to keep me destabilized, as if sincerity is in itself cruel, and has a gun pointing out of it.

It's a technique from old gay times, with a modern spin. I have never learned this trick, maybe because my way of dealing with the prospect of being bullied was to turn my light down so low I wouldn't stand out.

But he sees me. He must think I'm wide-open, an innocent who hasn't been around the block yet, like so many others in Town, and that might be true, but it's also not. I don't carry myself with a lot of certainty. Perhaps in my J.Crew chore coat, I have the air of someone who's fairly clueless in terms of how to dress as a Creditable Gay. I must look like a person who wants something, wants it terribly. I'm still capable of being enthused; I'm prone to blushing, the feeling that flushes my face and turns my feet the iciest cold, even when I'm wearing wool hiking socks. But I'm without a direction, having spent the better part of my twenties in grad school. I've been made a baby by deadlines and grades, being told what to do by school or by my father, but a baby can't fend for himself out in a tough world like this, where people need to make up the rules on their own, day by day, or else they die.

And is that why he wants to hurt me a little? Break me?

He says something about my ditching the straight-boy clothes. He's going to take me shopping, tell me what to buy, but not today. He has a better idea in mind.

After a walk back to the Work Center, we head up the stairs to my apartment. He steps behind me as if he's been up there once before, but I doubt it. Maybe he sees that sex isn't an easy, casual thing for me every time, and that makes the prospect of what we're about to do more exciting. We pull the shirts over our heads and step out of our pants, kicking them away. He isn't afraid of being expressive, of saying the lusty things from a place deep in his throat, not his usual speaking voice. I've never been with anyone like that. He becomes a bit of a rough animal, and it's a relief to be here, not in the world outside but in the place of dreams, where we transform death.

And now, every other guy I've had sex with? In retrospect they all seem timid, held back, probably reluctant to look slutty.

Slutty: bad word in these years. Slutty gives you sickness, slutty makes other people sick. Slutty makes you die, even if we know you could practically be Saint John of the Cross and still manage to seroconvert.

Slutty is low-class, which is possibly the worst thing to be in the United States of America.

We're just lying on my bed after a while, his head on my chest, looking out at the room. It occurs to me that I might be afraid of him, as I've been afraid of everyone I've ever been attracted to. They seem distant, unknown to me, which is probably the very trait that attracts me to them. I'm not so much afraid of them walking away, leaving me behind—I'm strong enough to survive that. The fear lies in my self-perceived inadequacy, and that fear seems to shimmer and thrive in the gap between us. My psyche, my libido seem to require this gap, and if I can't perceive it, then, well? My interest isn't there.

We have a routine. The gray station wagon pulls into the Work Center parking lot, and instantly I step away from the window so he won't see me looking—we pretend to be casual. I am sure others look out their windows and say, Yes, that is Hollis's car, and all is right with Paul. At other times, I go over to his place, where we take off our clothes in the cold and slip down into the hot tub behind his house. The hot tub feels transgressive, because he has a boyfriend. Not that Lou lives there, but what if he should happen to stop by to do a load of laundry? What would he make of the towel I'm drying myself off with? Lou isn't always so nice to me when I run into him around Town. There's a bite to his friendliness. "Oh *really*?" is his signature expression, which he wields when you're comfortable with him, and in your skin. The two words together suggest bemusement, dominance: Aren't you a precocious semidelightful simpleton? He takes you out of your present, takes you out of your power. Still, we talk to each other as friends—and honestly I do like him and want him to like me. He wants to hurt me only so much. If he hurt me too much, he'd reveal how jealous he actually is and thus lose his dignity, his power. How can he be possessive if he and Hollis have an open relationship? It would violate some pact. He would lose a measure of control if he allowed those feelings to show up in his face, to color the tone of his voice, though I'd be surprised if there weren't blowups about their arrangement (maybe even about me) in the late hours after they've watched a movie on TV or come in from the hot tub. If the blowups aren't directly about that issue, then they might show up in terms of who had left the hot tub on.

Their arrangement, which insists on trust and is meant to keep trouble on the periphery, probably ends up putting trouble front and center.

Certainly Lou can tell how much Hollis and I are drawn to each other. He must see it in my face, he must see it in Hollis's, though Hollis as always comports himself to show that deep feeling will not get the best of him. Not that Hollis is cold or numb. No, just the opposite. Hollis is always warm and lively, eager to laugh heartily and play, even if that playing involves making a joke when things get too serious. It's like being in a kayak going downstream, and Hollis jerks the route of the stream abruptly, and goes out into the bigger harbor without telling you. Sometimes I want to say, Can't you take anything seriously, dammit? Social life is absurd, yes. The manners we make up are nuts. You and I know that. Does that mean all of our reactions must be absurd? But in Hollis's way of seeing, we are never to take ourselves too seriously, especially if our lives—our entire community—could be lost tomorrow.

I suppose Hollis would know about loss. Hollis had had a long relationship with Jaco, another man, several years older. Jaco is involved with someone else now, a younger man. Jaco and Hollis are still friends. Jaco has AIDS and is not doing so well. He's in and out of Beth Israel, and Hollis must be in some pain about all this, even though he'd somehow manage to alchemize this pain. Maybe he wouldn't turn this pain into a joke, but maybe he'd be all too willing to insist on the everydayness of it, as if he and Jaco didn't deserve better and more. And thus he'd have no reason to feel rage.

Welcome to homophobia, or what we do with it, how we turn it against ourselves.

I honestly don't want to hurt Lou, though I know I don't care about Lou's feelings as much as I should. I wish Lou would see us, in the largest sense. I wish Lou would step out and away, and find someone closer in spirit to him: someone equally feral, outlandish. I don't doubt he loves Hollis. He's possibly still in love with him, but really? It's impossible to imagine him being devastated by the loss of Hollis. If that weren't so clearly the case, then I'd certainly, well—back off?

In summer Lou dances most nights at Ryan Landry's House of Superstar, where he is a go-go boy, and one of his signature moves involves bending over, grabbing his ankles, and showing his asshole to the crowd, who feign the indifference of the sophisticated. The asshole, a ridged, deep pink, does not look exactly friendly. The asshole asks you to deal with it, accept it. The asshole speaks its aggressive thoughts out of a north–south oval. It's almost too much to look at, but I do so for a second, then look away again. I might cry. Lou spends Tuesday nights away from Hollis, at his own place, where he presumably spends nights with his own friend with benefits—or does he? That butt is about to blow up in our faces.

Twinship

To go on living a full life which includes sex, in this time of AIDS, is an act of resistance. I believe we resist because we simply will not give in.

VIC D'LUGIN, "Power & Passion"

In Hollis's lexicon there is no higher term of endearment than *dick pig*. Not everyone gets to be called a *dick pig*, and I consider it a supremely high honor to be described as such. There's something pleasing about the way he tosses it off. *You're part of a club. You like sex, it's one of your gifts, and you are not inhibited with decorum or fear or good taste.* Those words rinse clean the stigma, the shame of total immersion and commitment. They also take away the complexity I've always associated with sex. I don't even mind that they siphon death out of it, as if death were never sex's twin.

9

Recycled

It's not just that the sun sets so early; nights are longer in other places: Reykjavík or Fairbanks. It's just that eight o'clock can feel like two in the morning; Town isn't exactly timed to a forty-hour workweek, which means it operates more intuitively, in tune with the animals. But some of us still carry the energy of our former urban lives, and cannot stomach the idea of crawling under the covers at 9:30 p.m., even if we've written hard or gessoed canvases all day. On one particular long night, I look around my apartment for something to do, but it's not there: every sheet picked up and folded, every surface dusted, cleaned, scoured. There is a single can beside my sink waiting to be recycled. I pick it up, walk down the stairs, and intend to carry it to the other side of the parking lot and drop it in the recycling bin. At the same time, my downstairs neighbor's door swings open. In Tim's hand is a single can. He's about to do the same thing. Our laughter can be heard all the way to the dunes. We'll still bring up that story twenty-five years later, as if it manifested the excitement of winter nights.

Butch, Butch, Butch

In a matter of weeks, I am no longer wearing my gold J.Crew chore coat. In fact, I'm no longer wearing *any*thing that could be found in that catalog: the ubiquitous costuming of my twenties, the look of inclusion and aspiration, but also the look that once allowed me to disappear. Ludicrous! Shirts with collars, button-downs, khakis, boat shoes—*out*! Or else pushed to the side of the closet, in resentment. Whom was I trying to please? It's no small deal to take on the look of a subculture that's still derided as dangerous. Not here in Town, but a few towns south, or off Cape.

It's surprising how quickly I take to this new appearance, as if my body had always been waiting for it.

Today I have on an olive T-shirt, skinny white jeans, a blue bandanna on my head. My sideburns come down into points, dark facial stubble clipped in the blunt approximation of a goatee. Hair buzzed on the sides, and a long, wavy, romantic clump on top. I wear Doc Martens even though they hurt, not just a little but a lot. They are likely a size too small for me, and occasionally a terrible clear bubble on my heel leaks and burns, keeping my sock disconcertingly wet. I could either buy them from the shoe store in Town or drive all the way to Boston, and I don't have time to drive all the way to Boston. I must be like my mother, who claimed her feet were ruined in childhood because she didn't *know* shoes weren't supposed to hurt. I decide I will never wear an outfit that doesn't in some way insist: Butch, butch, I am too butch to live. I become a different person inside these clothes, and for the first time in my life, I understand costuming not as a falsehood but as a way to bring the inner life out in the open. Turning myself inside out is another way to put it. Why keep dreams to myself when others are all too ready to be actors in them?

Hollis and I shop for a motorcycle jacket. I pick up the first one I see, slug my arms through the sleeves, shake my shoulders into it. It feels good. I'm as much at home in the jacket as someone who's never even stood within fifteen feet of a Ducati could be.

Hollis shakes his head from side to side, eyes half-closed, chin lifted. A slight smile establishes his position, his knowledgeable position. "Too roomy, too big."

He might actually say it looks like a housedress on me. A muumuu.

I stand before the store mirror, which elongates me, confusing my sense of my body more than ever. The houselights are bright. It occurs to me I still might like my clothes roomy and big. I'm not exactly a muscleman eager to show off his arms, his tight butt, his chest as deep as a chest of drawers.

It's curious that I give in so readily to Hollis's instruction. I don't say no to his advice, and don't experience it as an act of control. When others in my life have attempted to control me I have not responded so well, and have either pushed back or walked away. As much as I'm wary of power, I appreciate instruction—it's pretty clear Hollis has my welfare in mind. And I have a pretty strong sense that Hollis doesn't perform this role for everyone. Again, I feel chosen by him. He wants to mentor, as someone must have mentored him once, as no parent, no school teaches you how to be a queer person. And you can learn only so much on your own, especially in these last days before the internet.

When I get back to the Work Center I beat my brand-new jacket against the stones in the driveway. I beat my shoes too—no hiding. Again, Hollis's advice. "What are you doing?" Marty asks. "I am making it wearable," I say, and the look on his face suggests that he completely gets why I am doing it: he is a visual artist, after all, and understands spectacle. I beat them to suggest that the new is wrong, a sham. I beat them to suggest that anger belongs in the spirit of my clothes. I beat them because—am I angry at Hollis? Because he means so much to me and isn't as available as I'd like him to be? It's not the year for perfection and the ideal fit. At this point in time we are only damaged, scraped, burned, and used.

Boots & Battered Jacket

My mother meets me at the gate of the Tampa/St. Pete airport. I'm happy to see her, she is happier to see me: I only wish the laugh that comes out of her mouth did not sound like it's protecting itself from shock. Whatever I'm wearing—I must be embodying some fears she's been brewing. She looks at me as if I am wearing a costume but she won't tell me to take off the boots and battered jacket. That laugh is a way to put me in my place. The scolding inside it—the dressing down, so to speak—familiar: it's fed by the culture in which she grew up, in which you don't stand out, you don't look like you're having too much fun, you don't make too many claims about yourself (as much as she would probably like to wear a battered motorcycle jacket too). There's practically a voice in the expression on her face: I have lost my son for good. Which contains shades of hurt, betrayal, horror, and confusion. She's beginning to let go of me, as if she can already imagine some brawny Bluto buggering me from behind, about to fuck HIV into me. If she lets go of me now, it won't hurt so much when she has to do it later.

The Big Beast

There's a spectacular feeling that comes from being seen as desirable, especially when I'd never thought of myself as being desirable before. It has a rightness that I experience deep in my body. It shapes the way I stand, the way I speak, the way I assess a situation without equivocation. It's energizing, this feeling. Boats go golden in late light, clouds rush forward, as if in the wake of a tropical storm. A relief: now I'm just like other people. I don't need to eat, don't need to sleep. And yet I feel distracted and achy, too, as if I've just come down with a mild ongoing flu. My mind cannot even be still long enough to fix a confused sentence, and I'm in part relieved when I have an excuse (dishes to wash! I have to pee!) to leap up from my desk. If this is love, I'm not sure I want it. Love is too many lines of coke, your mouth dry, the center of your head aching and ice-cold, and every nerve in you alive, so alive.

Hollis must feel a version of this, too, but if he does he keeps it sealed off, away from my sight. It's tough not to resent the hiddenness of him, what he values and doesn't, the complex and negotiating math of it. But in hiding his emotions from me, he's teaching me to keep feelings in perspective when they could so easily take on a life of their own. A big beast is prowling through my life. I imagine he doesn't want the beast to prowl through his, too—not at the same time. He's lost enough for now, not just Jaco, but so many other friends I can't even tally. We've all lost a lot, even if we haven't loved or known the dead ones around us, and it would be no surprise to be told we are acting out. But acting out is for people who have a safety net, and queer people have no safety net, unless we're protesting for our lives, in the big city, en masse. We're acting on our feelings. We're at the edge of the world, and you say this isn't a time for indulgence?

Transmission

Would AIDS be a different beast if you could catch it from the air-conditioning, or by a sneeze or subway pole, a public swimming pool? Back in the '80s Reagan didn't even mention the word, not even when his wife's best friend, the famous Hollywood actor, went off to Paris, skinny, ugly, exhausted, scared, for experimental treatment. We know exactly how you get it now—we know it requires multiple exposures. But transmission is associated with what? Parts of the body—*acts*—some people don't want to talk about. Not frottage, nothing polite or gentlemanly. But more often than not: sodomy. The ass: site of shame, even for the most sex-positive kind of person, though they'd never admit to that. All those internalized phobias that the ass should not be used for sex when the ass has been used for sex since the beginning of time. The ass isn't always clean. It's unpredictable, unwieldy. It has a mind of its own even when you believe it's emptied and clean.

As if disease itself is smell. Or vice versa.

The hovering stink of judgment, the slippery mud of its dream. Not just from others, but from inside yourself. You've brought it on yourself. You let in what your body was never supposed to have. This is what you get for giving yourself too much freedom.

This is what they've done to us.

10

Scrub

Am I angry? It doesn't occur to me that I might be one of those people who turn their anger inward, against themselves, to make it look like another emotion—inertia or loneliness so I don't have to think of myself as an angry person. But why am I opposed to the anger in myself? Why can't I make a home in it? Is it just that anger lives in absolutes, slams the door on nuance? Is it only that anger doesn't always feel so good, like running six miles without any of the endorphins? Maybe it's just that anger wears me down, and when I'm in a fury I don't have the distance to think through a problem and then I'm back again in the house of my childhood, listening to my raging father, and I see how weak it makes him, hear how it turns him into an idiot, no captain of himself, and then he's using it against my brothers and me. There we all are, in the middle of the night, installing a new kitchen at the shore house at three thirty in the morning, and everyone except for him is pretending to find it funny, Aren't we the craziest family, because it's easier to laugh at madness than to say, No, this is wrong to us, we should be in bed now, sleeping. We should be taking care of ourselves, replenishing, brushing our teeth now, drinking water. We could resume first thing in the morning. But anger filled every glass in our house. We drank so deep of it we were convinced it was sacrament.

He called my brothers and me into the bathroom. It was always one at a time. You never knew when it would be your turn. He'd be in the tub after a long Saturday of work, the water around him dense and gray, as if it had been expelled by the laundry room hose. The project was to scrub his back, not with a brush, nothing with a handle—that would be too safe, not personal enough—but with a washcloth. It was always the cream-colored washcloth that was already discolored, rough, cheap, with torn edges. The air would be too warm in the bathroom: a swamp with a dome over it. A smell of soil and dead skin and mist. Did he want us to adore him, adore his body? He must have known that there was nothing to adore of his back, red and freckled from repeated sunburns, with a small white crater near his meaty right shoulder, as if someone had once punctured him with a screwdriver. It was not about getting us to love him. Rather, he wanted his skin to rub off into us so we would not forget the cost of everything he did to give us the life we had. The martyring. And if that isn't anger in its purest, most frozen form, then I can't read the world.

George & Martha

Fighting between my parents is always out in the open. Fighting never hides. Fighting is behind and ahead of us, roiling beneath the bed or out in the kitchen drawers. There's nowhere to go to be safe from it: the barks, the shrieks, the slammed doors, the snapped-off syllables. From a distance, the fighting might sound so absurd as to be from a comedy. Years later, my brothers and I will crack each other up when we mimic certain lines, but when you're in the thick of it, there's nowhere you can go to shut it out. Your hands aren't big enough to cover your ears. It always feels personal, this fighting. It always feels as if it's about you, as if it started with your own birth.

It gets in through all the openings in your body: your pores, your nostrils, your ears, your pee hole, your asshole, your mouth. And when they're yelling, how can any other sound come in and find you? You can't tell where you begin or end when that sound is in the air. No one is blameless, no one can walk away sparkling and clean, even after the doors have been closed and the rooms, though silent, are still ringing. You smell gamy to yourself, as if you haven't worn deodorant. And is that why your mother says, "You have B.O.," when the two of you are alone in the car, on the way to your music lesson in Cinnaminson? She says it as if she likes you less for having a smell, for leaving childhood behind, for the possibility of leaving *her* behind.

The tantrums are so full-bodied they feel like sex, or a substitute for rough sex, actually—an instinct it takes me years to put words to, but why make your children your prime-time audience?

Why not put your children in another room, tell them to play out-side and cut the back lawn with the noisy mower—*some*thing? It makes sense that my brothers and I watch *Who's Afraid of Virginia Woolf?* with awe when it comes on the TV one night. George and Martha, Hump the Hostess, we didn't need to understand what the fighting was all about. We knew it as music, which might have explained why my mother walked out of the room fifteen minutes in; she couldn't stand seeing how it comforted us, made us laugh so hard, made us feel less alone. She didn't need to hear the sound of her own voice echoed back to herself.

11

Three Ways

I'm slowly learning that there are three ways to be a queer man, socially. I could be part of a pack. I could socialize as part of a group. I could disappear into the group, be a listener in the group, and it wouldn't matter from the outside—I'd still be one of the chosen. I could be the person I never was in high school, or even college. From a distance this might look like a lot of fun, but my fun might only be group-bound. I might not be able to slip away. Might not be able to leave with the dark-eyed guy looking at me from the other side of the bar. All my group members concerned with every flicker sent my way. Or every one I send out? The possibilities of evaluation, dismissal, mean jokes, jealousy. Group as cockblock. So I lose the possibility of sex, and drinking (or drugs) becomes my sex. Groups are evolutionary. Groups have their roots in starlings, in murmurations, snapping above the landscape like a scarf, dense as ink at the corners, then thinning out in a flash, but that doesn't mean every creature has the gene to be a part of one. I know I don't have that gene. Perhaps I still have a kind of PTSD from gym class.

Or I could be in a couple, which has obvious benefits: comfort, reliability, routine. Others gravitate to me now. It's safer to approach a pair, less threatening than to talk to a single man. I might not fully know it, but others are trying to read the roles in our relationship. Who's the quiet one, the talkative one? The bottom or the top, or are we versatile? Do we have sex, or has that long stopped between us, and are all our alliances outside? Who makes the money? Who makes more? How does that shape how we stand next to each other, whether we look at each other's faces to lend support when the other is talking?

But there's nothing like walking into a busy room as part of a couple, nothing like that statement of love, of identity. In a way I look more gay than I would if I were on my own—much more so than those who are part of a large group, who could even be mistaken for frat boys, gregarious to the point of aggressive, their public expression no longer simply about sex, even if they are walking around shirtless, with tight jeans.

Or I could be on my own, what I'll call the Lone Man. His first preoccupation isn't with finding a boyfriend. He isn't romantic in the traditional sense, but is romantic with the world. Though lonely, he knows there is value in his freedom, in his ability to pack up at any moment, whether for a trip or to start a new life. He can have sex, lots of sex, if he wants to. And the sex can always be an adventure, as it isn't friendly, married sex. He looks forward to the challenge of walking into any social situation. He has to be awake, has to be looking. He cannot afford to sleep in any social situation, for he can't depend on a sidekick to do all the work for him. He must play both parts, all parts, and so he is often extra-vivid. Some try to match him with their best friends, or else shake their heads at what they see as an inability to grow up, but he knows better than all that. He has learned how to say no to outside pressure. He knows how to take care of himself, as he doesn't take his confidence for granted. Maybe he was once in a relationship and he knows the cost of being involved with someone, giving up a part of his identity to someone, the danger of losing his boundary, losing too much.

The Provincetown of 1992 is a friend to the Lone Man, who is always more queer than gay. His status comes with no stigma, unlike in other gay communities in which group affiliation is insisted upon in public places. The New Boy is a Lone Man, and in that he sets a standard for everyone. All kinds of cultures, queer or straight, human or animal, tell us our value is determined by the packs we run with. The Lone Man has himself.

Wrenching

I am walking down Pearl Street with someone I don't know very well. Maybe because I don't know her very well I am at more distance from Town, the structures I've started to take for granted— only a stage set for the people up inside their rooms. The yards aren't thick with dark, jungly plants, no ceiba, no mahogany, no flame of Jamaica, no silver buttonwood, none of the plants that crawl and twist through the novel I'm working on, the tangled flora and fauna meant to conjure up an atmosphere that's personal. No, I'm right here. The stars overhead, the rooflines, the pitch of the eaves above the window peaks. The blue hour, holding on as long as it can before night. "If I had a boyfriend . . . ," I start, then close myself down before I can complete the sentence. I go back to where I was. There is no reason that wrenching beauty should be enough. In that moment beauty is all about death, and my friend knows that too.

Intuition

Hollis's legs stretch out across my lap. Winter chills the moisture on the windowpane. The sun hasn't shone in days. There is a possibility of change both outside the window and inside the room, which is hot from steam, visible in shadows, rising off the radiator fins. I can't actually give words to it just yet, but it's an intuition I feel deep into my feet. Sex won't always be like this. By that I mean people won't have to rein themselves in, cordon off certain acts. They won't look at a drop of semen on a chest as if it contains spilled nuclear fuel. Sex won't always be intrinsically wound up with dread, with the possibility of accident and error: blood going into the wrong place, a bitten lip, or through some membrane so thin it's barely a barrier.

And when the right drug comes along they'll be obsessed with semen for a while. Every aspect of sex will be about fetishizing it. All sex will be toward making contact with it, as if sex's sole purpose was in service of that contact. They'll want to taste it, they'll want to rub it all over their chests and faces, as if it might ward off bad luck. Then one day they'll get bored with this obsession, realize how peculiar it was to turn what has always been human essence into danger, taboo. Maybe they will even get tired of sex, as sex will be everywhere, at any time. Sex will be like running, or stopping at the supermarket's salad bar and filling up a cardboard container with leaves.

Does danger make sex more erotic? Would I find it so compelling if I didn't experience it as a bit of an obstacle course? If it didn't have within it the possibility to kill me, if not now, then five years from now? Would I feel this ache? Would I be missing something?

Fucked

At some point in February, when it's still cold but the days are getting longer, Hollis says, "You're staying for the summer, right? Where else would you go?" As if I've already been ruined for the world. Like no one else I know, he makes pronouncements like that with such certainty they leave no room for doubt. He says such things with an amazed laugh, which suggests years and years of crazy experience. The Town of summer, or at least the way he describes it, doesn't sound exactly like fun. Overwhelming to the point of sickening, but necessary. The Town I'm getting to know through the off-season is only a dress rehearsal for the true experience of it. Or maybe it's just getting its sleep and taking its vitamins. In recovery mode from what came before.

Does my decision to stay happen over time, or is it triggered by Hollis? I really don't want to live anywhere else. Else suggests duty, denial, safety, patience, routine. Else involves desensitization, suppressing disrespect, brutality, inequality. An emphasis on numbers, statistics, positions. *Commerce.* Trash along the roadsides and overpasses. Stalled traffic at red lights. People harried in supermarkets. Else does not involve a conversation with water. Else does not have a sense of extremity, life-and-deathness in the air. Hollis is right. Town has already written itself into me. It's fucked me in the manner of a lover, and I might as well just get used to sharing his bed, though I'm not sure I want to be in his bed all the time. Is that the ideal life, and I'm just too controlling, too invested in the values of my former life to give in?

And yet how do I know freedom isn't weakening me? Could inclusion and acceptance make it harder to return to the world I've left once it's time to move on? I might become one of those people who haven't crossed the Sagamore Bridge in years, someone who forgets how to tie a tie, or gets too used to outfits that are more costume than anything. Outfits that might look juvenile and needy under harsher, more jaded eyes.

And money. Who doesn't struggle with money here? Who doesn't live in an apartment that's too small, no closet, an under-the-counter refrigerator? Who doesn't worry about the cost of electricity, the cost of heat, how much water you put down the septic tank? Not to mention the work season, which lasts all of four months, mid-May to mid-September. Two jobs, fourteen-hour days, at best one day off a week. If I rent a place for the summer alone, I'm required to pay the full amount of the term before I've even moved in. My two fellowships are close to running out. They've allowed me to be comfortable, more comfortable than many of my friends. I get to go out to dinner in February, I get to pay for my friends' meals. But what will happen next year?

Days pass. I know what I've decided but it takes me some time to announce it to Polly and Hollis and everybody else. I will find some way to live. I will do all the necessary adult things. I will no longer carry the built-in prestige of being known as a Writing Fellow, but I've moved beyond caring about the rewards of all that months ago. I will be *among*, in a way I haven't been before. It's a new thing to be among: all my life I'd thought my only choice was to be extraordinary, as if to compensate for some lack. There is freedom in failure; I know that—how could I think otherwise after living with the body's collective breakdown? Maybe it's art enough to try to build a life against that breakdown. Maybe that's enough.

12

Escapes

Although we know it's our home, we also know our home is remote, surrounded on three sides by cold water, over an hour to
anything of use. We have an overlarge new supermarket, a few
convenience stories, a few doctors' offices, a handful of restaurants
still open, a gym, a few garages, two thrift stores, but other than
that? We are as remote from the real world, as other humans call
it, as Nantucket and Martha's Vineyard are remote from the real
world—they might even be closer, with their ferries. So when
either Polly or I say, out of the blue, "Cape Cod Mall?" we might
as well be proposing a trip to the Caribbean. We're embarrassed to
admit it to others, but sometimes we miss the brute and ruthless
practicality, a deep need that cannot be satisfied in Provincetown,
with its fidelity to the local. (Chains, with the exception of the
necessary A&P and Cumberland Farms, are legally outlawed in
the town of sexual outlaws.) Maybe this urge is about touching
back to our pasts, Polly's in Kent, Ohio, mine in New Jersey—
the business strip of Hyannis, after all, does not look radically different from either. Or to put it more precisely, maybe the break
between our past and present feels too strong, a false binary, an
ersatz compartmentalization that could only make anyone crazy,
the way my father's departure from Allentown, city of his birth,
made him crazy, racked with guilt. Or we are simply trying to shed
adult responsibility, the hovering stink of illness, the sickness of our
comrades from AIDS. It's good to be part of Town, but it's good
to leave Town for a few hours, and as soon as we hit Wellfleet,
ten miles south of the border, we are Hansel and Gretel in the
woods, looking for compelling sights to catch our eyes, whether
it's a church thrift store, the herring run in Brewster, the tidied,
idealized Cape Cod of Chatham or Dennis or Yarmouth Port, a
fox trotting through the grave markers of a Harwich cemetery.
Edward Gorey's house on Strawberry Lane. We make up characters,

hold extended conversations in their outlandish voices, and crack each other up. Some of what we make up might be truly funny and inspired. Much of it isn't, and we find that funny too. We propose a scenario in which Polly goes up to the counter of a drugstore and says to the cashier, with a pained look on her face, "Excuse me, Miss? *Miss*? I have feminine needs. Emergency?" It's not menstruation itself that makes us laugh, but advertising, our anticipation of the clerk's prim, alarmed reaction. This is what happens when you've lived long in a place without taboos, where you've become too used to seeing someone with AIDS-related dementia walking down the middle of Carver Street, buck naked in winter but for the sheet around his shoulders, which is horrifying, but simultaneously funny.

Needless to say, the scenario remains proposed and stays in that space.

It probably takes all of an hour. We suddenly feel like travelers from some cordoned-off tropical country, and the real world starts to lose the crackle of novelty and becomes closer to what it is. Even though Polly is straight, she, too, is already weary of a world that appears to be built in support solely of procreation and generational stability. A world of the whitest white people, with no room for difference. A world in which queer people and artists are way off to the side, if they even exist at all. The lights in the stores hurt our eyes. Our mouths are dry, our psyches like pieces of felt to which someone has taken a needle and started scratching until there's no surface left. We haven't eaten enough. And we're low on protein, on hydration. Our eyes are full of looking and looking at too much junk, at stuff that doesn't even merit our attention. Is this too much immersion and our senses are drained? Have we wasted valuable time? We just want to be back home, but we don't feel like driving the long route back, two lanes most of the way, not just the thirteen-mile stretch of Suicide Alley, but the speed trap of Eastham. I can see the tiredness in Polly's face, the left corner of her mouth weighted, the spot between her brows knit tight and tense. I'm sure she can see tiredness in mine. Something has turned. The milk has soured, too much time in the car, in front of a heating vent or defroster, too much time trudging back and forth across parking lots, slamming car doors shut, and driving to the next lot with weeds growing in its cracks. In people's faces you can see the cost of taking on several low-paying jobs in winter, living off unemployment or Social Security checks. Food on the cheap side, kerosene heaters in the kitchens, all for the sake of living near the precious ocean and dunes. Polly and I think this is the real world, but for these people, this cape is their escape; this is their Provincetown. We come back home with flannel shirts or sweatshirts we might wear only once or twice before they drop to the bottom of the drawer, take on the smell of mothballs or camphor, only to be donated to Ruthie's at the first sign of a crocus next year.

Only when the Pilgrim Monument comes into sight do we sense why we have left Town. We're lucky to have visited the world. We're even luckier not to have to live in it.

Dutch & Farsi

On quiet nights like this, I think, I should call Denise, my oldest friend, whom I once talked to every day for two hours. I tell myself to pick up the phone and then I decide to put it off until the morning. Is it just that I no longer have time for long analyses of the people who aggravate and mystify her? Not just that. When we try to talk now, all we hear is distance in our voices, and it hurts at either end, I can tell. She's living in a suburb some would call upscale, in a restored house with a high-end kitchen and restaurant-sized stove—and I am, where? What could you compare to Provincetown? I'm talking about a place where it's impossible to speak a sentence without folding death inside its structure, and when we talk, we hear two different languages that can't be bridged—for now. It will change later, but that will take years. The single time she comes to visit, she steps off the plane as if she's dressed for East Hampton, by which I mean expensively, with high heels, gleaming hair, and makeup, and when we take a walk on a fire road toward Truro's Highland Light, she talks incessantly about boyfriend troubles without lifting her head to see the trees, the cliff, the immensity beyond. Squint a bit and you can't even tell the sea and sky apart, the lucent blue is exactly the same. It goes from the bottom of the world to the top. And that's as close to a sign as I've ever been given. No binary, no division. Why won't she see?

Maybe it is too painful to know there is another life when the life she has needs to mean everything.

Skyscraper

I imagine Denise's words upon stopping in Boston after her time in Town:

So many tall buildings.

The awe and dizziness of looking up, as if she has parachuted back to earth after being dead for so long.

13

Imbued

> Queer ephemera, that transmutation of the performance
> energy . . . function as a beacon for queer possibility and
> survival.
>
> JOSÉ MUÑOZ, *Cruising Utopia: The Then and There of Queer Futurity*

To make something beautiful is a radical act, especially when bodies are decaying, splashed with red spots as if a paintbrush were shaken over bare skin. The bartender at the A-House? Legs so swollen from KS, each leg is the circumference of two legs. None of the doctors and nurses have seen such a thing, so they wrap them in moist rags, which doesn't relieve his pain. Richard Baker paints a red tulip. Someone might think it's merely a flower, but he's looking at a body, maybe even a specific part of the body, a penis, a nipple, a throat turned inside out. Same goes for the waterfalls falling out of one of Polly's heart paintings. It's a body that knows how close it is to the precipice and maybe that's why it coruscates off the canvas. José Muñoz again: "Queerness is not yet here. Queerness is an ideality. Put another way, we are not yet queer. We may never touch queerness, but we can feel it as the warm illumination of a horizon imbued with potentiality."

Taxonomy

There isn't a name for what Hollis and I are for each other. Someone could say we are friends. The word *friend* is capricious, its very sound is warm, inviting: it has the potential to contain many dimensions. And yet it feels like dissembling to introduce him as "my friend Hollis," as if he's merely a workout partner, a study buddy. My anxiety over this matter might compel me to drop his name more than if I had an actual category for him. Do I simply want to own him? Or do I want to be owned by him? Neither of these options sounds satisfactory without the other, but then again I wonder if intimacy and attachment are even possible without the roof of a category.

As much as I claim that categories are restrictive in every other realm.

Hollis uses the term *fuck buddy*, but that seems simple, malnourished, as if we are just two teens getting together after soccer practice rather than two grown men in their early thirties. It diminishes, it builds tight walls, and it doesn't even give us any space for fondness and affection. Does Hollis think about his fuck buddy late into the night when he can't sleep? Does he grab on to his pillow with his arms, or put it between his legs and think about how deeply he'd sleep if the fuck buddy were lying next to him, resting his head on his chest?

The two of us are walking up Pearl Street toward the Work Center. These days the sun goes down at four. Often you can feel the light starting to dim after two, which does not gladden my spirits, especially today. Another moody day: the sky never left darkness behind. My writing isn't going so well. That doesn't mean I'm not trying, just that I have written only a handful of scenes in months. They are possibly on-the-way-to-good scenes, but I can't seem to grow the novel before and after those scenes. I'm agitated into my deepest layers. Suddenly my desire to be simply *among*—to be just another Provincetown queer—isn't enough. It pales against what every human wants: purpose, recognition, contribution—attributes that could possibly have significance beyond the day we're in. For the first time in my life I have been living for now, against futurity. But for today at least that isn't enough for me. I have been working on two novels at once; I have been working many years, and to turn my back on all that now? Well, that would be crass. It would disrespect all the people who have read my work and pushed me and counted on me.

And what if I'm not around in two, three years? I doubt that I'm dying, but it would be callow to be too certain. A sickly child (mononucleosis, mumps, chicken pox, speculations of leukemia and cystic fibrosis), I learned early on to be attuned to my body, to what hurt, to the parts that felt tired, achy. I do not think I'm sick, and though I could take the test, I'm apprehensive. Why be tested when the drugs they have are useless and damage the body? Is that the way to live a longer life, a better life? AZT, Bactrim, DDI, Retrovir, aerosol pentamidine: names out of science fiction films that don't even evoke comfort, but have a violence in them, as if to remind us that the disease requires an ongoing vigilance: guns, bombs, and knives to keep a genocide at bay.

But maybe the disease is stealthier than anyone's ability to out-run it. I will simply wake up one morning. I will reach over for my glasses on the night table, put them on, expecting the usual miracle of sight. I will not be able to see. I will try to blink blink blink the darkness away but I will be like the narrator of Sebald's *Austerlitz*, who thinks he knows what's at stake years before his book is out in the world. "Even when I glanced up from the page open in front of me and turned my gaze on the framed photographs on the wall, all my right eye could see was a row of dark shapes curiously dis-torted above and below—the figures and landscapes familiar to me in every detail having resolved indiscriminately into a black and menacing cross-hatching."

My Lie

Occasionally an acquaintance asks me if I've been tested. Once, I say I am negative, as if this person, a casual acquaintance, wouldn't be able to bear it otherwise. If I told her the truth, it might might even be an occasion for a lecture. To which I could respond: All the sex I have is safe sex. And see her looking right through me, as if she can see right into that night with Billy, our two bodies lying side by side on the bed.

I haven't seen Billy in so long. Someone tells me he isn't doing very well.

And I can't get my mind off my lie. It is the one and only time I lie, and though I excuse myself by saying that people of good char-acter do bad things at times of extremity, I don't like to meet this part of myself, as maybe this part of myself is unstoppable: a creek run over the banks, flooding neighborhoods. Why would it be so much harder to say, I don't know? I'm afraid. I want to live a life that isn't focused on my health, on prolonging my life, or on avoiding my death. I want to have as much freedom, and opportunities for trying and failing, as you do. I want to have the privilege of being bored. I don't want to endure the smells of a doctor's office, or the repeated sticks of a syringe. I don't want to get used to the sight of my blood, or a tongue depressor. I don't want to wait by the phone for my latest test results, shuddering when they're not what I want to hear. I don't even want the adrenaline of good news, because that's always followed by a physical letdown: fatigue, depression. I don't want to lie awake at night, thinking of my doctor's face, whether I'm still handsome enough for him to feel attracted to me, as absurd as that sounds.

I want some control, even though I know that not dealing with the future is a fiction of control.

Let the day ahead be a bowl on the table. I will fill it up with want, and let there be nothing beyond that to measure. Until the next day.

I'm not ready to be old now that I've just become young. I wasn't young for so long, even when I was five years old.

Then again my agitated feelings are probably too big to pin to any one explanation. Lack looms on this cold, moody afternoon. Lack pools and settles into my bone tissue, the empty shops and restaurants on the streets. On other days lack is on the periphery. Lack is bearable when it isn't right in front of me, in the center of my vision. On this day all I can see are piles of oiled sand on the street, unswept steps, side yards unmown for years, a doormat curled in the middle of a lawn, broken flowerpots turned on their sides, the dead marigold stalks still crisping and colorless. Town does not look loved. And if people do try to love Town enough, wind, rain, salt, sleet, blowing sand, and snow will do their part to undo human efforts.

"Look at this street," I say to Hollis. "The houses on this street. Did you ever notice how fucking ugly it is?"

"It's not ugly," he says, laughing, denying my perception the way my father routinely does. We keep walking, silent. And for the first time ever, I hear just a shadow of doubt in his tone. He doesn't sound so sure of himself and is perhaps startled that I've been so blunt, as it is out of character for me; he's known me only as agreeable, pliable, sweet. And maybe he senses I am not talking just about how people take care of their houses, but about us.

Or maybe my disillusion is just the necessary turning point. I'm no longer a visitor, but I'm becoming somebody who's putting down roots. It's taken four months to turn my past to blank, unremarkable terrain, not unlike that moon up there.

Seal

I can't sleep one night. A tree casts its shadow on the ceiling. I feel the branches of that tree in my body, as if it's grown into my ribs. Will I wake up one of these nights, cold, with chattering teeth, sheets drenched in fever? Will I find rashes on my side, on my face? Will I look up at the ceiling and think, What if it's in me? I try not to think of the metaphors of political paranoia, but I can't get them out of my head. Why did I wait so long to attend to this? Why do I still wait? Could that encounter with Billy all those months back have sealed my story?

Musicale 1

On a cold night in February there's a benefit to raise money for art supplies for people with AIDS. Billy is both the curator and the Johnny Carson of it. The house is full, every ticket sold, and with each reader or performer, Billy's face gets prouder, brighter. He can't hide his enthusiasm and his love for us. It's one thing to come up with the idea for a fund-raiser, but something else to pull it off, especially at a moment when his health isn't so great, and several people in the audience, his closest friends, are visibly struggling. Hardly any event in Town takes place without somebody leaving to attend some health emergency. Off to the side there are two men in wheelchairs, docked close to the exits in case they don't have the stamina to stay.

The two Michaels read, Mark reads, Marie reads a poem.

Kathy: first time she's read since Arnie's death. Face shy.

When it's my turn I read a bit from *Bad Florida*, a novel I'll soon put aside for good, although I'll always know it as my first novel. A woman and two children, one her son, the other kidnapped from a boyfriend, are escaping from home. Their departure is anything but easy. They have loved their house, loved the place where they'd hoped to spend their lives. It's 2 a.m., long past their usual bedtime. They're escaping Chick Keatley, a former astronaut, with Halley, the man's disabled daughter, in tow, heading to Golden Gate, Florida, because there's a cinder block house there and it's cheap and they don't know where else to go. They're in the convertible with a hole whistling air through the top. When Natalie, the mother, sings a line from *West Side Story*'s "Somewhere," I sing-speak it in my own voice, quiet, deliberately awkward, and a shade under pitch, instead of reading it, as I do the other text. I want to make sure it's not pushed or asking for feeling. This isn't about whatever wisdom and sensitivity I've been able to catch; I'm long past disappearing into my role. *There's a place for us, somewhere a place for us.* I don't yet know that those borrowed lines are more important to the audience than anything else I could have read. I don't know till the evening is over that I was singing about AIDS.

David Sedarisness

In the car one day, Hollis puts on a tape of a guy named David Sedaris, though he won't be David Sedaris for years. Some of his stories crack me up, especially the one in which he talks about his lover Bruce Springsteen, and other guys whose straightness is never in question, but the work as a whole doesn't get under my skin the way I want it to. It doesn't make me feel dangerous or nervous, and as soon as I admit that to myself, I listen only toward trying to identify what Hollis sees and hears. The humor, of course. The proud badge of geekiness—*expressiveness*—as a way to manage absurdity. Hollis tells me I should write like David Sedaris, which sounds like he believes my own work is not funny enough or else he'd be putting *my* book on tape into his tape deck and we'd both be driving down Route 6, spitting out laughter against the windshield. But David Sedaris is good because he's found the David Sedarisness inside himself, brought it up through his fingers, and typed it out. David Sedaris wouldn't have listened to the person who told him he should sound like, I don't know, Phyllis Diller? I keep that to myself.

Responsibility

Oh, it's more than just a good time. Sickness doesn't exist out here, in this space, in this pocket of an hour. Out here we can pretend to burn any sickness out of our bodies, out of the bodies not even on the floor, or near.

It's actually the best time when it's just me and some of the other Fellows. The middle of the week, minutes before midnight, and as soon as we step onto the A-House dance floor, we claim the space as our rec room. The temperature inside is far less feverish than it is over the weekend. In spite of the roasting fireplace, the room is not such a sauna with only a few of us here; it's calm and comfortable and dark. Bodies stand on the sidelines, along the bar, green beer bottles held at belt level. The music is Yohan Square. Nobody needs to work too hard. We're not about merging, nothing so simpleminded or cohesive. We're stepping in a single line around the perimeter—first parodies of wooden soldiers, then robots. We don't have any responsibility other than to illustrate that we are heads, arms, legs, cocks, cunts, assholes, belly buttons, fingers, tits, feet, hands, butts, elbows.

14

Bubble

Summer is as wonderful as it is awful. Week by week, through June, the crowd builds. Then it's busy, always athrum, a buzzy, elongated hive stretching cells from Pearl Street to Franklin. The street is quiet only after 4 a.m., when I'll see a lone guy walking home from the Boatyard. By the time August rolls around, every single human, plant, and animal is shredded, abraded, overwhelmed, overstimulated. Nerve endings rubbed with steel wool. We're too exposed, and each perceived aggression makes us snap and lash out, bewildered that we're harboring that much rage—what the hell is wrong? Aren't we in the most beautiful place in the world? Could it be all that salt air, which corrodes the bathroom faucets, skins paint from the wood? In the West End a moving car almost pushed me into a parked car, and I'm a storm: a whirling comma spitting acid and wind, like the ongoing storm that shapes Long Point, out where an abandoned town, Hell Town, used to be. The driver turns out to be my friend Mary, sweet Mary, who sticks her head out the window, with a concerned look, to see whether I'm all right. The voice coming out of me? It is not a voice I'd want any other human to hear, much less someone so kind, funny, and down-to-earth. I tell her I'm sorry, so sorry. I don't want her to think of me as the bonehead who talked to her like that. Luckily Mary seems to forget instantly, and when I bring it up a few weeks later she casually calls herself the shittiest driver on the Outer Cape.

And in spite of all this, time floats. Time just floats as if we're all above the earth. Town a lyric bubble outside past and future. Town a dream that rips up all your intuitions about narrative and goes its own way every time I think the arc of a story is here. The sun goes up and down. High tide and low, restaurants, bars, head shops, sex shops opening and closing—how could I not be aware of the tide when the Town beach is all but swallowed up twice a day, water all the way up to the tops of Town landings? I'm not living my life the way other people are living their lives. Town summer is an experience of being fully present, no dead minutes, no burned patches of grass. Looking out at people, being taken in and evaluated by people. Not much actually boring. Do people go crazy when their lives aren't boring, when they're part of an endless, ongoing movie? I'm in a state where I'm close to feeling high all the time. While I know a few people who might like that idea more than is best for them, my brain wants something else after weeks and weeks of it. Maybe it wants rest, dullness, darker colors, sepia. No light or bodies. No voices. Inky night. Cool water. A lobster buoy? Raft floating on stillest harbor, five hundred feet out from the breakwater, 3 a.m.

A Lion

A floating piece of space, a place without a place, that exists by itself, that is closed in on itself and at the same time is given over to the infinity of the sea.

MICHEL FOUCAULT, on the boat, "Of Other Spaces:
Utopias and Heterotopias"

On holidays Commercial Street is a bit like an old pinball game. It shoots me out into obstacles and then bounces me back through the flippers, knocking me against silver knobs that light up and ring with multiple bells. On one hand it's safe. I don't have to compose myself the way I would in other places. No possible queer basher is going to follow me down the street. No one is going to scowl and call me by a slur. My shoulders fall backward; I lift my chest upward and out. I bare my arms. I can be a lion here. And just when my body agrees to that feeling, a car comes up right beside me, too close; the driver wants me to know he has places to be. Hear the revving engine? A truck lurches by, its sideview mirror just grazing the top of my shoulder, not enough to hurt me, but just enough to make me cry, "What the fuck?" The trucker has no clue. He has crates of beer to drop off, and if he stopped to worry about everyone on the street, he'd never get this cargo unloaded. His daily stress is ten times more than my daily stress, and at the end of the day he has to drive all the way home to West Yarmouth, forty-seven miles away. But you can't keep to the sidewalk when it's just wide enough for one person, and people are walking in both directions, and people stop to say hello, to encircle a Great Dane who rolls seductively on his side for public inspection.

Would I really want a peaceful street? While that sounds like a reasonable thing to ask for, maybe all that safety would lead me to sleepwalk through Town. If I'm worried that a handlebar is going to hit me, or a truck's mirror is going to box my ear, I'm going to stay awake.

Administrative

There is an opening for an administrative job at the Work Center, and once my fellowship runs out, I pounce on it. The job involves not only janitorial duties, say, cleaning apartments and helping the grounds manager move an occasional mattress, but also administrative office work. In the office there are just two of us: Liz, who runs the operation in summer, and me. There's enough work for a dozen people, but this is a period when no one expects to get anything accomplished. There are larger matters around us to get stressed-out about. The office itself looks half-finished, wood overhead and on the walls, some of it raw or painted white, wires and extension cords hanging. My office chair barely held together with corroded screws. Nabi, the Work Center cat, makes a satisfied nest out of our workplace. Sometimes she's up on a desk, sometimes down on the floor in an afghan throw from the '70s. I'm not even aware of all the flea bites I have until I go out to solicit businesses for the center's upcoming summer auction. My ankles sting. They're so red they look like they've been stippled, and I can't help but pull up my pant leg and scratch myself, as I ask a B&B owner to donate a free weekend to us. He looks down at my scratching, frowns, then relaxes his face. He scratches his ankle, too, and signs the form with near-perfect grade school penmanship.

4/4 Time

It's hard to keep my mind on the body on top of me, on my own pleasure, the hand on my throat, my chest, my dick, his dick. Should my mind be on my pleasure or on pleasuring the person I'm with? Is there a morality to sex, or are all ethics off the table once I'm lying flat on the bed, just as long as no one is getting hurt? Should I be close to my everyday personality, should I laugh and talk? Should there be breaks? Or should talking be kept to a minimum—how else would I shake off the straitjacket (no pun intended) of self if I weren't leaving language behind? How could language in such a situation be anything but porn language, secondhand, trite, shop-worn, embarrassing if I saw a video of myself, and someone were sitting there in the room to watch it with me?

And if all that weren't enough, when I'm in it, even if I might be enjoying it, I might be thinking, When will this be over? I'm not sure if I like how this feels. Am I hurt? How long do I put up with that motion before I decide it feels like—like—surgery? Should I say stop? If I say stop, am I changing the course of our time together? Will my stop make you—me—self-conscious, too concerned about how we're feeling rather than our pleasure, as if the two were radically separate categories? Do you have to involve your teeth like that? Is it OK to let a tear roll down my face? And yet—sex that is too comfortable, sex that doesn't change—well, what could be more boring? Sex that is concerned only with getting *you* off, sex in 4/4 time, all plunging and stabbing with no variations of time signature. No wonder women (and some men) pretend they've come just so they can get the whole procedure over with. Why would anyone ever stay in sex—risk the disappointment of it—if not for the dream of falling into a new net, being cradled by it, taken to a place to which neither of us expected to go? Carried in space, caught just above the current of the abyss.

Foglifter

Other times the devil is a ghost and he's taken something from me, or turned me into a ghost with him. His kisses fill me with a cold gas and then take the cold gas out. And then I'm only an empty membrane, without shape, a broken balloon. Something has been taken from me that's not exactly flesh and bone, but what? All that's left is the fog of me. He's stolen something. And that was always his plan: to use me a little, to leave me with less, because he's not concerned about self-esteem. He feels better if he leaves me with less. And I've let that happen. I've given him that power. He's preparing me for the hardest things, and I still think I can escape aging and endings. Maybe I should be grateful to him.

And at other times I could just use a big, fat cock.

Phone Date

My mother picks up the phone just when I think she isn't going to answer and I'll have a reprieve. It always makes me ache to hear her hello, the particular cloudy color of it, as if she's just downed a glass of milk, an old habit from growing up on a dairy farm. Sometimes when I'm first talking to her, just before I catch myself, I go right to that place when I was in camp in sixth grade. Her voice is as familiar to me as blood, even if I'm working harder than I should to sound cheerful. Lately I've been putting off those phone calls to her, only because our conversations make us feel further and further apart when we're trying to draw closer. It's as if she's still speaking English, and I've left that old language behind. I don't even understand its verb forms or articles or syntax anymore—is that why there are so many pauses and breaks in my sentences? I tell her I'm having a wonderful summer (which sounds like I'm rubbing salt into a burn), but there's so much I can't share with her. She hears it. And into that empty space she spills so many generalities. It's as if she's trying to close me down rather than draw me out. She doesn't want to hear about my nights out. She doesn't want to hear about Hollis or being knocked off my bicycle or dancing on the stage at the A-House. So instead she talks about Pebbles, our family Boston terrier, who got bitten by a pygmy rattlesnake last month when the two of them were out for a walk one night. But I've heard this story before, detail by detail—and how has she forgotten I already know? It worries me to hear her talking like that. It makes me feel awful to remind her, Yes, I know all

85

about Pebbles's snakebite. Do you think I'm that far removed from the family? Tones slide into tones we didn't intend. A tone sounds like aggression, and once we name it as such, we can't refigure the conversation, which must disconcert her as much as it does me. For so many years we finished each other's sentences, and now we speak with the politeness of exes, of a couple who's had a terrible falling-out.

Finally, to break things up yet again, I tell her I have news. I tell her that I've gotten a Second-Year Fellowship at the Fine Arts Work Center. I will be here through next May 1.

I tell her that I have just found out, when I actually got the news weeks back but was too apprehensive to tell her. Once, my mother got excited by my good news. She reacted as if the award or publication or reading was as much for her as it was for me. Now, though, she hears the announcement with wariness, as if the purpose of such awards is to take me away from her. I tell her it is extremely rare to be given two fellowships back-to-back. They are open only to present and former Fellows, the competition is fierce, they are very much coveted, and though I know it sounds like I'm bragging, waving the flag of my good fortune, I am simply trying let her know that home is here, I've come to know myself here, I can't go back.

She tells me she's happy for me. I can hear that she's trying not to sound hurt, agitated. It's taking a heroic effort. That does not stop her from saying, "Does that mean you're not coming home next year?" But I can bear it. She's trying to envision days ahead without company, nights before the TV, just her and the dog, cooking for herself, lost in her worries about the past, about what is to become of her if she falls down or if she's had a stroke.

"Daddy should come down to stay with you. When is he coming down next? Why's it taking him so long to get the Cherry Hill house ready?"

"Your father—" she says. "You know you can't push your father to do anything."

"Really? I think you can just be more up front about it. Forthright. Just say it, dammit."

"Well, *you* talk to him," she cries, as if she's just said a curse word.

We talk some more. Her trying is almost too hard to listen to. I hear the aspects of martyrdom, and I can't stand the way she's so ready to give herself over to the role. Why not say no to it, why not resist? If no one resisted, even the current president would never say: AIDS. And yet it would be a mistake to overlook the fact that behind her hurt she's still excited for me, proud. That pride isn't calculated or false, or even very much about her. There couldn't be a parent prouder of my achievements—there she is after one of my first public readings at Rutgers, walking up to me, unable to contain her laughter, her face wet with joy—and yet no parent wants to lose a child, even if she doesn't quite know what that loss involves.

15

Wally

Wally is warm, funny, brown-eyed, handsome. He has the demeanor of a much younger person, a great big boy inside a man's body, with a deep urge to visit the absurd, which is part of a greater urge to laugh and connect. I have gotten to know him through Mark, his partner, on Pearl Street. Lately his health has taken a turn, his tiredness keeping him bound to the couch for days, though he still has that glow to his face. He can no longer work, which he used to do with Polly at Pennsylvania Company, the clothing store at the center of Town. All of this is complicated by the fact that Mark must leave two nights a week to teach at Sarah Lawrence, in Bronxville, just north of New York City, a drive of five hours, 280 miles away. Wally needs someone to look in on him, not anything as elaborate as cooking or cleaning, but just to sit with him for a couple of hours, and Mark asks if I would like to do that. There is a small stipend involved. The money would not come from Mark and Wally, but from some Visiting Nurse Association fund. There is already some in the account, and it makes sense to spend the money if it has been allocated.

But the money part makes me a tad uncomfortable. Shouldn't I insist on sitting with Wally for free, as I would if Polly were sick, or Hollis were sick? All sorts of people in Town, queer and straight, have been stopping by to check on their neighbors for years. But money inscribes a boundary. Money ensures I will show up when I say I will—on time, present, ready to help if need be. Money, even if it is a little money, will remind us of how grave this illness is when we'd all probably rather run away, sick or not sick.

If Wally gets the best treatment possible, well—it's quite possible he could live for a very long time.

But before any of this can happen, I must be vetted by someone in charge of the program. Her name is Nora, and she can't interview me over coffee downtown. The usual reference checks will not do.

No, she must see my house, must see how I live, even though Wally will never come here. It isn't expected he'd ever come here.

The times are so extreme, it doesn't even occur to me to question the ethics of her visit. Though some pay heed to established routines and procedures, others still make rules up on the fly, day after day. This is an emergency, more deaths than ever in Town. What health professional has time to mourn anyone? The names of the dead fill a big book, and not a few of the doctors and nurses hate its existence. They run on autopilot now, and the big book is an invitation to mourning, but an invitation to mourning has the weight of a threat now, as people need to keep themselves closed and strong as a way to keep going.

My studio apartment at the Work Center is admittedly not the finest. The back wing of the cottage I'd spent my fellowship in. Sky-blue wainscoting, wallpaper of tiny red roses, long bathroom off the big room, which is overtaken by the bed. A narrow kitchen complete with a coppertone wall oven, so many layers of grease on the floor tile, around the cabinet handles and the electric stove burner plates, I'm not able to get any of it fully cleaned. In truth I haven't done enough to make the apartment my own, to make it look loved. I see it through Nora's eyes as she stands beside me. Her job is to ferret out the possibility of fraud, any person who might get the idea to use state funds in improper ways (drugs and drink). Because of that she is conditioned to expect the worst of people. As we attempt to converse, I can feel her scanning my place. Her eyes pretend to be on me, but really she is using them to imply judgment. She's thinking: Too small, depressing. She is waiting for signs of a bong or a load of porn to topple out. The person who lives here is flailing, not on the right track. I'm sensitive about her judgment because it others me, it's what poor people must feel all the time when law enforcement demands to come inside. Nora does not think of me as an ally or peer. She does not even see me as a writer, or as someone who went to grad school. I am queer and thus a failure to my gender, to the dream of white masculine power I choose not to serve. She has worked around plenty of queer people, but she makes it clear, through strategic references to her husband and children, that she isn't one of us. All kinds of people break rules, sneak in unapproved medicines through the back door of the clinic, and as if to counter all that rebellion, Nora clings harder to the rules and bureaucracy. I suppose I'd have more compassion if I could see we all need order, we all grab on to it in our own frustrated ways in times of deep chaos.

I know this kind of judgment is happening everywhere, in much harsher terms. And I'm getting only the gentlest taste.

And yet I'm approved, readily. I've gone through my hazing and I'm to stop by and see Wally on Tuesday afternoons.

I walk through the garden, come in through the kitchen. I'm told I don't have to knock. A bell hangs from the back of the door, rings, and Arden, a black curly-coated retriever, barks and rumbles up to check me out. "It's good," I say to him, and sink my hand into his fur. "All's good. I'm just coming for a visit. I'm so happy to see you."

Up until this time, I have seen Wally only up and down Commercial Street, Wally in the garden, hairy Wally in drag. The Wally I have known has always been eager for conversation, eager to speak in that baritone voice, which is surprisingly gentle and fatherly, as if his voice box were made for singing. Not the way men sing now, straining their voices into androgyny, but the way men sang in the 1940s, like Perry Como. But Wally is quiet today, lying on the living room sofa beside the two windows almost smothered by rose vines. Light barely gets in. It doesn't seem like he much wants to talk—or even can today. The lamp is on beside him. *Wheel of Fortune* blares on the TV. Arden sits by Wally's sofa with a look of worry in his eyes. It's as if he decides the very arrangement of us, our two defined roles, sick one, well one, have conspired to make Wally feel worse.

I've known plenty of people with AIDS, but this the first time I see the illness's less dramatic repercussions up close. I try to get past the feeling that I don't belong here, that I'm an imposter among the sick and the grave. This role is for people with actual experience, better kindness. I ask if he wants anything, needs anything from the store, but Wally doesn't. The situation is puzzling: I'd feel useful to go out and get him some, say, chocolate fudge brownie frozen yogurt, but Wally has no appetite and doesn't want me to go out of the way.

"It's only just down the street." I point in the direction of the L&A Market. "It's really no trouble."

"Nn nn," he says, shakes his head back and forth on the pillow.

So I pull up a chair and we talk. We talk about people in Town, people we think of as funny, people we approve of, people we don't. There is a transgressive thrill in taking down a member of our community whom everyone professes to like, is required to like, and we talk of his narcissism, his meanness and aggression—can he even dole out a compliment without a firm backhand on it?—with relief, as if we are the only two people on earth who have ever spoken the truth. In effect, we are saying we like each other. We think alike, we trust each other, and if only our conversation were happening in relaxed circumstances, on the steps outside the post office, or the bench outside Spiritus, the main pizza place in Town.

He'd make the perfect boyfriend at a different time and place, and I sense he can see that in my posture and expression.

When these topics run out, I find myself bringing up my crushes, my failed dates. I fear that I am talking too much about myself, or more precisely, the objects of my desire. Am I conjuring up too much hope? Is talk of desire talk of hope? What are accounts of longed-for boyfriends, and all the awkwardness, all the attempts to connect, if not failed stabs at hope? But maybe it is better simply to be distracted, to get lost in the channels of narrative than just to sit here together, in time, to feel it flooding over us, like we're on the banks of a lake after a hurricane.

I wonder if I ever allow myself to take in how afraid I am. It's hard to admit that I am waiting for a catastrophe. I haven't yet lost anyone close. Uncle Joe, of course, when I was a teenager. Uncle Steve, Aunt Anna. My high school friend Paul to diabetes. Plenty of people, but not close people. The loss of someone close still feels like an abstraction to me. It happens to other people, and I feel embarrassed about it, the way I feel embarrassed about not knowing how to be fluent in other languages.

We never talk about Wally's health, how his body feels this week, if he has headaches, or if his feet hurt. To go there would be to etch something he might not want known, even to himself. So sometimes we just sit together in silence, the lamps on. We listen to the steps outside the window, no car noise or tourist noise to bandage those sounds. We look to see who it is—a carpenter with an awl in his hand? a Visual Fellow drawing in on a cigarette, swallowing back a cough?—while Arden lies fully on his side, looking up at me with one eye, legs stretched as far as they can go, as if he's trying to fill the room with himself.

The White Dory

An opportunity arises in which the Work Center will subsidize my rent each month if I can find a place off the compound. I grab it without hesitation and find a winter rental in the far East End, as far from the center of Town as possible. I tell myself that no group experience could equal the group of my first fellowship year, and I don't want my second to be a letdown, to be one simply of comparison. But I think the real explanation is deeper, and more disturbing to attend to. My psyche is likely more exhausted than I'm willing to admit. What right do I have to retreat? But just the idea of a sound-free world, of snow pinging the windowpane—a life frozen for a while, suspended as in some paperweight . . . well, all of that seems as blissful as a fireplace on a night that's so cold.

The new place is on the second floor, with a tight view of the harbor through one of the living room windows. I must look out and over the roofs across the street, one of which is Norman Mailer's house, the other the Motherwell compound. I'm anxious, though, about the electric baseboard heat, the price of which could possibly be enormous, far exceeding my housing stipend. Dee, my landlord, probably knows what she is doing by escaping to Key West for the winter. Even when she's fifteen hundred miles south, it is impossible not to think about Dee at all times, as her paintings are on every wall, colossal scenes of the ocean. But they look redundant in this space, given the harbor across the street. So much for the limits of representation. With care and great guilt, I take just about all of them down and stack them in the second bedroom, which I've closed off and turned down the heat in. Dee is a tiny woman, with a tan speckled throat and arms, even in the off-season. She does not like a wide range of food, period. She winces even at the very name of the Box Lunch's Organic Pocket, a vegetarian roll glued together with mayonnaise, so it is no surprise her paintings are so big. She is making her body so small and has to attend to the opposing impulse.

It doesn't take long to experience the shaking—the whole structure shakes when a 35 mph gust hits from the north, which proves to be unsettling in a place already built to withstand high winds—don't some call it the windiest place in the world? But the bigger problem involves clams and gulls. The roof, which is nearly flat, a fifteen-degree peak, proves to be the perfect canvas for gulls to break open clams on. They take them from the beach and drop them from a height of thirty feet, with a force like bombs. One day a clamshell is dropped right over one of the skylights. It cracks the glass and tears a hole open to the sky above. Drafts of cold air blow through the hole, underneath the flapping blue tarp, which threatens to blow off like a magic carpet until the glass can be replaced.

How long does it take me to figure out that no one lives in the White Dory in the off-season? Not just here but in this end of Town? The place is but a five-minute drive to the Work Center, and another five minutes to the A&P and the gym, but in terms of walking, or even taking a bike? Figuratively, it feels as far from the hub of activity as Braintree does from Boston, and in order to resist the isolation, I'm out for much of the day. Beneath me lives the painter Emily Farnham, a former student of Hans Hofmann and the biographer of Charles Demuth. She's so eager for someone to talk to, so relieved that a new tenant is living above her that I cannot help but feel her aloneness, despite her smile, her wry, enthusiastic voice. At eighty-one, she's outlived all her friends, and she's unthinkably alone out here. We have great conversations when we run into each other on the steps, but I find it hard to get away once we're talking. She seems to want something I'm not sure I have it in me to give. Not just taking down a bowl from a high cupboard shelf, or moving an ottoman from one end of the room to the other, but something psychologically costly—am I thinking about my mother? That's it—my mother. When I see Emily's gray Volvo station wagon crushing the oyster-shell parking lot, I make sure to stay inside for a while, even if I've packed my bag to go to the gym. I wait till I hear her door close; I wait a full five minutes, even more, then I walk out down the steps, as quietly as possible. I do not like this about myself. Perhaps my own fear that, like her, I'm going to lose everything makes me hide.

Funerals

On the long walk to the UU Meeting House people linger in groups of twos or threes, solemn, too well dressed for Provincetown. Their heads are lifted as if it's work to keep them up. The mourners are young and I don't even have to know what kind of funeral it is. I walk a little faster to my destination, just so I won't be pulled into it. Not just a conversation with somebody I know, but the energy. I'm rattled into my psyche and soul, which I don't want to admit, even to myself.

I've never even been inside for one of those funerals, maybe because no one I know would approve of all that fuss. Maybe it's just that the people I know aren't attached to family and big groups of friends, and to hold such an event under those conditions—well, that would be sad, too unbearably sad for the few who slid into the pews. I'm relieved that I haven't yet been summoned to any of these rituals, but I know I'm not participating in an experience of Town, of this era, that's too layered for me to comprehend. One day I won't have a choice—could it be Billy? Philippe?—and I'll be fused into Town's history in a way that I'm not now.

In the meantime I picture my own funeral taking place in that—church? No, the UU Meeting House refuses to call itself a church. Not next year or the year after, but someday. I know it so deeply it isn't something I ever discuss, not even with the people closest to me. I realize I take it for granted that they'll be there to sing the hymns I'd have picked beforehand.

My shepherd is the Lord. Nothing indeed shall I want.

16

Welcoming Committee

It's October 1, and I stand out in the parking lot with Tim Seibles, the new writing coordinator, watching the new crop of Fellows move into their spaces on the Work Center compound. I probably have the face of unsettling calm, as if I'm someone who owns and runs the place, when I'm typically Mister Anxiety. Tim and I are making jokes with the effortless silliness of those who have been standing out in this parking lot since before anyone had given a thought to paving it. Maybe with our laughing we are hoping to set the tone for the new year. We cannot help but feel, on some instinctive, unspoken level, that we are an unlikely pair of friends: Tim is black, I am white; Tim is straight, I am queer; and maybe we hope the new crew sees our joking around and ease as a sign that people from different backgrounds can be together. Not to dissolve that difference, but to love that difference.

A blondish woman walks up to us and introduces herself as Lucy. She doesn't meet Tim's eye, she doesn't meet mine. I feel the history of every reaction to her face, simultaneously, from both men and women. She's standing up to meet ours. She knows it so well by now that she's probably not surprised by any complicated gaze—and she's strong. But the three-second silent dialogue among the three of us—the deep pocket in time—feels more charged than it should. It's as if she has jumped into my head and decided that I've decided that I don't like what I see, and it's animal and primal—and also not true.

Lucy is beautiful. I'm not even sure she knows that about herself, as much as she might directly say to herself: Yes, I am beautiful. Perhaps her forehead, her brow, her hair, her lithe, athletic body only call more attention to the small pocket out of her cheek. It keeps the corner of her mouth drawn in as if she is trying to hold sound inside. At the same time, she has the aura of a star, someone who knows she's gifted, who's been much talked about. Word has it that she got an advance of several hundred thousand dollars to write a memoir based on a piece she wrote for *Harper's Magazine*. The piece details her childhood bout with jaw cancer and the numerous plastic surgeries she's undergone since. She's already a legend among her former classmates at Sarah Lawrence and the Iowa Writers' Workshop—we'd missed each other by just a year, and I have friends who are friends of hers. There's Ann Patchett, who was in my space the previous fellowship year, in which she wrote the first draft of *The Patron Saint of Liars*.

I've loosened up enough to see Lucy is wearing a motorcycle jacket, as small and as battered as the one I have on. She knows she is in Provincetown. A hank of blond hair falls over her right eye and covers at least part of her face.

In the weeks to come we become good friends. We defiantly believe in the possibility of love, sexual love, as a force that could transform us, and we are starving: we can never get enough. We find so much to talk about. We share with each other the details of our complicated love lives. But the friendship isn't ever as easy as it is with, say, Polly. The friendship is like walking through and around so many obstacles. Lucy has the ability to make me feel loved, seen—she knows how to shine her light on a person, knows how to use it. Lucy also has the ability to say something that hurts, then infuriates me, but I don't tell her that. Usually it involves stirring up competition about writing. She has the uncanny ability to locate and touch people's sensitive places, to say something provocative—does she like to fight? Maybe for Lucy prickliness is a gateway to intimacy, and she craves intimacy maybe even more than she does a hand on her face, her stomach, her hip. Alfred Kazin on Carson McCullers: "She fastened on many people as she did on me—for affection, encouragement, consolation. . . . She was also . . . ironic, devilish in her humor, circuitous in her dealings, charming beyond words when she wanted to be, irresistibly unique even when she drove you crazy." I don't even know if Lucy knew Carson's work, but truer words couldn't have been spoken of Lucy. Add to that some punk rocker's nihilism, an absolute disgust for complacency, sentimentality. Deep ambition. Lucy.

Matt, David, Alicia, Jane, Joshua, Mindy, Linda, Joy, Robert. In a matter of weeks it becomes clear that the primary characteristic of our new group is rebellion. Rebellion is an appropriate stance toward the times, when more people than ever are dying of AIDS, and the National Endowment for the Arts isn't funding performance artists who use queer themes in their work (Karen Finley, Tim Miller). There's so much to rebel against, it's confounding how to proceed, especially when we're in a place that values openness and acceptance and positions itself as a safe haven for sick people ready to die. So, in frustration, some target the Work Center itself. Why is it so hard to get a fellowship? Who was turned away? Why? There is an air of caution, incrimination, and wariness in our group. The possibility of fights, fallings-out. One Fellow, unhappy with her studio, throws open the doors on the coldest day of the season, turns the thermostat to ninety at a time when the Work Center is struggling financially, when there's a threat of stipends being slashed, maybe the threat of the whole operation shutting down, sold off as condos. At least that's the rumor.

My response to all this strife is to spend more time in my distant apartment than at the Work Center compound.

Elizabeth. Thank God that Elizabeth is a Second-Year Fellow with me. We were in the same class at Iowa, and it is good to have so many shared references, the same teachers, so many people in common. Dark-brown hair, dark-red lips, expressive eyes—when you first meet her you cannot help but be reminded of the young Judy Garland, without any of the craziness and need—and then that image falls away and she is just Elizabeth: no one else could be her. Besides, she is stronger and saner than anyone else I know. We enjoy making each other laugh, our humor so privately profane no one would know what to do with us. She is a brilliant writer, and part of that has to do with how her work's attuned to speech, the ways it lifts and pauses and breaks open in unexpected ways. Like Polly, she has a distinctive speaking voice that sounds like it was made for singing, though unlike Polly, she doesn't sing—she saves that for her sentences. It is good to see her back in a place she loves more than anywhere else. Good to know she's back in 6 Fish Up, where she gets the good work done. It breathes like a lung above the Work Center compound. It looks out on the buildings beneath and around it, but is not too much a part of it—you can hide up there and spy on the conversations at the two picnic tables on the green beneath and hear great gossip. She is writing a novel called *The Giant's House*, about an unlikely friendship between a librarian on Cape Cod and the tallest boy in the world. After that tough year away, she knows how precious time is and works with so much dedication that sometimes she must take a day off. She checks in to the Holiday Inn out in my part of Town, draws herself a hot bath, and starts up on the writing when she gets back to the compound the next day.

Elizabeth and I have a favorite T-shirt that appears in a shop-window in the center of Town: Knock It Off, Asshole, I'm a French Fry. Its accompanying graphic makes no sense at all, which is why we love it so, and our love of it has nothing to do with being stoned.

Aside from Elizabeth and Lucy? I fear I'm holding myself back from people, holding myself back from group life, which meant so much to me last year. But all that openness—I don't think I can do it again. Or I don't think I can lose it all again. I want to hold on to my vision of the ideal community, my utopia of last year. I can't afford to have it diluted. It would seem a sacrilege to dilute that, and so I decide to keep myself back from deeper, more loving involvement.

Imposter Syndrome

We're standing in the dunes one morning, where a famous pho-tographer is taking a group picture of the new crop of Fellows for the cover of *Provincetown Arts* magazine. We were told to dress in black. For some of us that's no problem. For others? It feels forced, an external idea of what an artist is supposed to look like. Lucy, for instance, decides to show up in a bright red jacket, with striped leggings. We're told to climb the crest of one of the dunes. One of us laughs; the laugh reminds me of how my mother laughs at me when she thinks I'm being pretentious, when my outfit doesn't match her idea of me, the child afraid of gym class, afraid of tak-ing a communal shower with the other boys, but too embarrassed to admit that even to himself.

But the photo isn't so much about the now. It is a photo about our deaths. It is a photo that is meant to be looked back upon, at a much later date, fifty years from now. At that point the Scandinavian seriousness of our faces won't look so self-impressed. No one will even think of us as posturing, so self-conscious in our glamour, as we'll all be dead. And death? Well, that puts us all in our places.

After the group photo wraps up, we stand in line, and one by one we approach the photographer's camera with all the gravity of young children getting ready to receive First Communion—or is it a firing squad? The smile I usually have on my face falls, and it goes instantly hard and very serious. Is this my inner life turned inside out, or just an expression of fakery, nothing much to do with me? One of us stands to the sideline, and like my mother, he laughs, a combination of disapproval, anxiety, and all the other inchoate feelings. Perhaps it's in response to so many faces changing on command. Or maybe it's just brute release. I feel exposed, as if he's thinking, That's not you. But there's no reason why I shouldn't be allowed to have more than one face. The other face, the smiling, welcoming face, is the face I make when I'm anxious.

I wonder what the Fellows in the brochure I studied all those years back would make of us now. Would they look at us if we were siblings, younger versions of what they once were? Or would they cry, Imposters?

Stay

> Cruel optimism is the condition of maintaining an attachment
> to a significantly problematic object.
>
> LAUREN BERLANT, *Cruel Optimism*

If I were Emma Bovary, I'd be trudging down Commercial Street through snow, in the middle of the night, ice caked into the eyelets of my boots, to see him. I'd bang on Hollis's door at all hours, I'd stand there on the step while his boyfriend answered the door, I wouldn't be afraid to shame myself for love, and as if to prove that, I'd reach down into the dirt by the doorstep, the part not covered with snow, the part where the dog lifts his leg, scoop it out with my hand, shove it into my mouth, and start chewing. I'd chew for the longest time without swallowing, biting the inside of my cheek, and once that mixture was mud, I'd spit it back out into my hand, and rub it all over my face. The boyfriend's gawking would serve only to heighten my ardor and anger, and to call attention to our dual plight, I'd rub some of the mud on him, rub it on his forehead, on his parted lips, rub it in spite of his yelling and flinching and attempts to jerk away, and scream, You're not getting out of this alive. None of us are getting out of this alive. Better get used to it, suckers, and only after I'd hear his weeping, his deep weeping, would I turn around, take off my clothes, squat, and pee in the middle of the yard by a cherry tree. I'd pee on the arriving officer, who would eventually try to handcuff me. Later, over at the police station, I'd pee some more, right in the plastic seat so I'd be soaking in myself, in my own warm broth. This is what love does to us, don't you see, you miserable fucking bourgeois cretin, and I'd collapse to the floor, collapse until all the rage was out of me. There's enough rage in me to fuel a nuclear power station, even if I had no idea what nuclear power is in the provinces of France, in Yonville, in 1856.

But je ne suis pas Emma. Hollis appears to have withdrawn from me, and by withdrawn I mean lost interest in hooking up. As I haven't allowed myself to be the one to initiate the hooking up, I am confused, as if I've been tossed up on some shoreline where I'd never wanted to be. Given that Hollis is in a relationship, I suppose I don't think I have the right to ask for what I want—is that merely out of guilt, a sense of being complicit in a scenario I must think is wrong? Is my gain at someone's else cost? But Hollis would laugh at the idea of guilt being for Catholics, who make his eyes roll for their backwardness and eager martyrdom. Hollis has never given me the sense that I should consider myself an equal—that's a condition I have agreed to, without quite acknowledging it to myself. I suppose if I asked, Shall we get together Friday after the gym? I'd be opening myself up to a rejection that might come too easily to him, offhandedly, as if there were a person inside me who couldn't be hurt. I hear how effortlessly, guiltlessly that *no* comes to him. It feels weird to be that tentative about us, especially now that something feels indefinably late about us being together. We missed something big, an exchange that could have heightened our lives.

Is it just that he has had enough change?

There's a Jack Pierson sculpture that simply spells out the word *STAY*, in found letters from a set of signs, so none of the fonts resemble each other. At another time that word would probably come off as safe and too cautious, but not now.

For all my insecurities, I'm very likely to pull away from someone once I sense I'm less valuable to that person than I once was. You don't want me that much anymore? Well, I'll show you just what you lost, son of a bitch. How do you feel about yourself now?

I would never have the long-term commitment of an addict. I would never know how to be an Emma Bovary: I'd never have the energy, never the faith, never the self-cruelty. Addicts don't stop. Addicts keep on going, walking right into the sun, in spite of the fact that they're burning up in its fire. They don't mind losing their minds, their perfect hair, their wrists, the skin on their fingertips.

I want to stop.

But that doesn't mean my abandonment doesn't scorch an inner part of me. It will take years to get the scorched part back.

FWB

We've crossed too many lines, Hollis and I. We make each other laugh. We know our parents' names, mimic their voices in character, hold conversations between his mom and my mom in which we talk about food, dishes, and where our kids went to college. It's no casual friendship: we can't even pretend that at this point. Plus, the idea of boundaries seems so safe. We don't even know what to do with that term, can't even translate it into action. If there are boundaries between us, it's that I'm not supposed to pick up the phone and call him. That's boundaries?

Sarah Lawrence Dancing

As it's a Thursday and not a Saturday, it isn't sweltering and packed on the A-House floor, so Lucy and I have room to move our arms without accidentally knocking anyone nearby. Not that the place is exactly empty, and maybe that's why Lucy dances with her pelvis so close to mine: I don't know what to do. I cannot hurt her feelings. She can have a tough surface, but I feel I'd wound her if I simply said, Stop! This is Sarah Lawrence dancing, not adult gay man dancing. The difference being that the first puts sex in quotes, and the latter? The latter keeps some distance between the bodies, because the possibility of fucking is scary, is real. And there are men looking on, not so happy with us.

Perfect

Somewhere in the world someone says *Provincetown*, and they say it the way they might say *Paris*. The tone has good intentions, but the deadly earnestness of it shuts its door on too many truths. It can try your patience when you've put in your time in Town. That voice refuses complexity. That voice leaves no room for any trait that doesn't support the myth of the perfect home: *There is a place for us, somewhere a place for us.* It doesn't want to know about full-to-capacity septic tanks or boredom or power outages or fights at Town meetings or the huge gaps between communities— any of the sacrifices and difficulties of those who choose to live in a place that's hard to get to, expensive to get to, isolated in summer, even more so in winter when fewer planes fly in from Boston, and everyone depends on two bus departures and arrivals a day. That voice doesn't acknowledge all the forces that want to make money from it, chew it up, spit it out. How much does it cost to rent the most modest retail space in summer? Thirty thousand? Sixty thousand? If I have to go one more night to free movies at the Whaler, where people scoop up free popcorn from a trash barrel, I'll choke myself. No wonder Polly and I take drives up Cape, lumping through the strip malls of dreary Iyannough Road in Hyannis. And then Frank Bidart stands behind the podium of the Work Center's Common Room. He reads his long poem "Ellen West" for the twenty or so people in those chairs, and his urgent voice is the inner life incarnate, and we wouldn't want to live anywhere else.

I'll never say Provincetown in that voice. The perfect world, the dream of: that's for people who want to stay where they are, in a place of routine and duty, which they don't have to inhabit fully. They need others to take their chances for them.

Acid Test

At least Benny isn't also dropping acid—I don't feel so soppy and timid. Happy Benny, who manages to have an edge, a sense of constructed urbanized cool, while still keeping his boyish country sweetness, even though I am sure he grew up in Boston or its suburbs. He looks like someone who might have had a recurring role on an Andy Griffith sitcom: the worldly nephew who comes back home to Mayberry after spending too many late nights at Warhol's Factory.

We're in the backyard of Hollis's house, where tabs of acid are being passed from person to person. There's no group pressure to participate, and I don't want to. I pass the cup to the next person. Maybe I want to hold on to some of my distrust, for without that distrust I'd have nothing to keep me tethered to myself. As much as I like some of the people at the party, I don't want to be just another bee in the hive. It takes so much work to be myself, it is ongoing work, and that's the way I stay alive, minute by minute. Without that, I'm the person I was back in my family's house, living in reaction to chaos, fearful, waiting for the next blow, a tumbleweed.

People in trauma give up individuality, which is made absurd by war, epidemics, poverty, racism. I look over at Jimmy, who might as well be blowing smoke off the end of a pistol. He is *Personality Supremo*. At least I have him.

We move outside to the deck, around the table. Leaves scratch the wood planks after a sudden gust of wind. Everyone seems unchanged to me. No one is climbing the roof to dive off into our arms, no one is staring long and hard at the nimbus around his hand, in the manner of a character from *Go Ask Alice*, the movie of the week, which was meant to scare the shit out of us and managed only to make drugs seem attractive and glamorous. Perhaps that pill is just a sugar pill and people are just performing their good feelings so that others will like them. Maybe it's just the public nature of this ritual that bothers me. It feels like a family holding hands and praying at a restaurant so others can see their virtue. It's never really about talking to God.

The Daddy of Boston

Maybe because he feels some regret about not being available to me, Hollis tells me about his friend Adam, a graphic designer, whom he describes as "the Daddy of Boston." It seems that Adam likes sex as much as Hollis does, probably even more. Adam likes sex so much he doesn't even have a boyfriend—how could just one boyfriend satisfy the voracious needs of Adam? Hollis offers to introduce me to him, and I say yes, yes, though Hollis cautions that Adam isn't to be thought of as boyfriend material. He gets serious about this: his eyes narrow and lose their sense of play. Is his sending me to Adam part of the ongoing sentimental education he's giving me? Or is Hollis still trying to keep my longing for him to himself?

If Hollis isn't in love with me, then he is definitely in love with my feelings for him.

The Daddy of Boston. Everyone wants the Daddy of Boston, because everyone is young, and all the queer men over forty are dead. To be the Daddy of Boston, you need to work out every day, maintain your musculature, drink your Dutch chocolate protein shakes, and live to be the ripe old age of thirty-nine. Somehow you've managed to escape the scourge of HIV, and that isn't the overt subject of you.

The very fact of you gives others hope: You have sex. You don't die.

17

X-rated

The new crop of Work Center Fellows talk about sex a lot, much more than if the Work Center were in Peterborough or Saratoga Springs. Sex is in the air, sex is in our work, it's changing our work in heightened, unexpected ways. One night, to stave off the off-season boredom, one of us decides to have a porn-viewing party—maybe it is Lucy. It sounds like an idea Lucy would cook up; Lucy is always ready to provoke and unsettle. As a group we have no intellectual agenda about this gathering. The intention is not to make any connections to the work of Judith Butler or Eve Sedgwick or any other theorist. Perhaps to do so would be to make this evening too safe. Nor is anyone out to stir up erotic feelings between us; our sexual desires are fairly well known to one another, and we're pretty much certain that what we're looking for is not to be found among us. But maybe Lucy is out to break down some boundaries. Her apartment sits out on the harbor, off the compound, and she has a TV and a VCR. Her living room accommodates a veritable crowd, eight of us. One of us is designated to go out to City Video and rent porn films: *Dress Up for Daddy*, a lesbian BDSM film; a film starring Long Dong Silver, reportedly a favorite of Supreme Court nominee Clarence Thomas; a film by Falcon Studios, featuring white, gay, gym-worked men; and a compilation of bloopers, terrible straight porn bloopers.

I'm not sure whom I end up accompanying on the trip. I am more than happy to be an accomplice.

Once we start looking our faces and postures change. The temperature of Lucy's living room changes. The occasional nervous laugh. We don't feel comfortable looking at one another: it is mysteriously unnerving to train our eyes to the actions on the screen, the mouth moving up and down on a dick, the eyes theatrically closed, the faces performing transcendence, ecstasy, submission.

Doesn't Sontag list "stag films seen without lust" as one of the prime examples of camp?

The gay film. I feel protective of the gay film, even though I know it's a bit predictable, orderly, and clean. The guys are white, swollen: striated, muscular. They look expensive. One is wearing a black leather vest, black chaps. These are intended to be props of transgression, but that is as far as the transgression will go. The guys are very serious about themselves. They look like the types who might tend bar down the street but never crack a joke. Each sex act follows the template of the day: small talk, a hand on the shoulder, leaning in, some kissing, some sucking, perhaps some gentlemanly ass-eating, a shy lick here and there, a condom is rolled on, howls and guttural noises, biting the thread count out of the sheets—you get the picture. The fucking looks vigorous and athletic but that's all it is: there's no passion, none of the awkwardness of human feeling. Nothing in the film embarrasses me: it looks like a hundred other films out there. I probably would never rent such a movie myself as it might be the gay porn version of Denise's high-end kitchen. No mess and the fires can be turned down with a knob. The moves are in style. The moves don't conjure up ideas of sleaze or bad taste. It's all polished and curated and maybe on the way to cold, not a body hair or blemish in sight. But what else should I expect in the age of AIDS, where bodies are getting prematurely old in the houses to the right and left of us?

My sense is that my friends are on the edge of bored. Maybe their boredom is a bit of a performance—the room might get nervous if any one of us, female or male, couldn't quite sit still. Yet I can also imagine no one wanting to offend me; perhaps they think I would take it personally. Cry out, Hah, homophobe! I always knew it. And start tearing up. There is certainly no revulsion in the air. But my friends seem disappointed, as if they were hoping to see something brazen, raw, and enthralling: just a single rough move to make them turn their heads away. Perhaps they were hoping that gay sex would show them something new about being human, about the inherent possibilities of the body, but no. The gay film has let them down in its dedication to ritual, which doesn't stop me from gazing at it with fellow feeling and pride, as if I'm a World War II veteran at an army reunion looking at footage of the invasion of Normandy.

No one cracks a joke. No one stands up to smoke a cigarette out on the back deck. Lucy still sounds excited, with a voice that wants to believe that the world is much bigger than the one we've been given.

Fast-forwarding through the rest of the film. I look around at my friends and think, You still like me? Maybe I am anticipating parental objection on a certain level. A different film is eased into the VCR, and boundaries slip. We're uncomfortable again, we don't know what to do with this language. There is a shade of danger here, some actual transgression: *Dress Up for Daddy.* Daddy in a movie filled with women? It is smart. Instantly it feels like a labor of love versus a commercial product. It understands a thing or two about roles and masks and the way desire makes use of projection screens, not all of them politically correct, most not. But alongside that it manages to be hot, no small thing when most of us in the room are not lesbians, or at least not yet. We are transported. We've all slipped into some interior state— there is a dream passing back and forth between us. We are breathing. The windows are steamed. What's that monstrous thing, a dildo? And while we might not all be aroused by what we see, we are absolutely in its grip. Whatever is happening has the power of mystery and subversion, but it manages to get there by the plastic, the fake.

But for Mindy, the lone lesbian among us, it's too much. The blush scorches her face. She leaps out of the room, onto the back deck, where she might smoke a cigarette—does Mindy even smoke cigarettes? I imagine her standing at the rail. I imagine her looking out at the harbor, moonlit and cold, trying to catch her breath, embarrassed and mystified by the intensity of her own reaction. While she's out there we worry together that we've offended her— has any of us said the wrong thing? Soon Mindy will walk back in with a nervous laugh, crossing her arms, rubbing the shiver out of her elbows.

We resume the night, in the hopes that the fun won't be spoiled by too much genuine feeling.

The bloopers film gets put aside almost immediately. Farts and premature ejaculations and running out to take a dump: it thinks sex is disgusting, thinks human bodies are ugly. It hates people, and was likely conceived and directed by someone who was never the object of someone else's desire, who never had satisfying sex in his life. We go instantly to the straight video. What is there to say about it? The actors here have done these moves so many times they can't help but rely on animal memory to get the work done; they're not at home, not in their heads, or in their bodies. They're not exactly bored but they're not so present either. Maybe some of them are simply drugged, but not on ecstasy or acid but in a K hole, which is another way to say: mild cat tranquilizer. Even I don't get unsettled by a close-up of a vagina. On the screen the vagina looks as friendly as a handbag, a pink one from T.J. Maxx. Maybe this is because the women are performing a kind of theatricality that doesn't align with their own pleasure, their inner lives. Rather, it is to convince the men, who are not especially dashing or endowed, that they are horse-hung studs, holding reservoirs of uncontaminated semen inside them.

The point hasn't been to vote on the best of the films, but as a group of artists and writers, we are obsessed with standards and we cannot help articulating our standards. A vote is cast. The winner? *Dress Up for Daddy*. Some venture to say it was the only hot one, and I silently keep my mouth shut about the Falcon film being plenty hot for me.

"I just want to be a lesbian," one after another of us declares, as if a dumb joke is one way to restore order and distance. As if there's nothing inherently patronizing about such a statement.

I will talk to Elizabeth about this night many years later. I want to know if I've remembered it correctly. How could any of that translate to an online realm in which we're always just one click away from porn? "Yeah, that was a bad idea," Elizabeth says. And we leave it at that.

18

Kenneled

Wally and I now know he isn't going to get up one day and walk down the street. He lies on the couch, I sit across from him, and conversation seems useless after ten minutes. I don't want to be a burden to him. And I don't want him to think he has to take care of me. What is time? I'm learning not to be nervous about having nothing to say, even though I occasionally fill silence with chatter. It would be better for Wally if I weren't nervous. So I sit cross-legged on the floor with Arden, who has grown accustomed to my visits. I let my hand get lost in the dense smoky black of his curls, which is as much about soothing me as about soothing him. Occasionally he gives tender licks to my fingers as if I'm broiled chicken.

Arden must wonder why Wally has stopped taking him for walks. And his confusion around all that might account for the fact that he's been eating so much. Whenever Wally cannot finish breakfast, he gives it to Arden, and as a result Arden has swelled to the size of a small household bruin. The weight puts extra pressure on his hips, his joints. It takes effort for him to stand, and he wobbles a bit when he carries himself from one side of the room to the other.

I probably don't know how much I am terrified of death, but I'm starting to sit with it. It would be unseemly to even mention any of this to Wally: he has enough on his mind. The only real gift I can give Wally is to pull us both into the here and now, when the future is looking at us, so loud and scary we can already hear it roar.

Wally doesn't want to say too much—or maybe he can't. He might simply want to keep silent so I won't know what he's losing. If he sees me see something lost in him, maybe there is reason to be scared.

Three creatures in stillness in the room: the furnace high, peace in the middle of catastrophe.

After an hour, Wally says, "Your check is on the kitchen counter."

And I always know that's a synonym for: I'm tired. I think it might be time for you to head home.

Paying a visit to my friend. Wally.

One Wednesday afternoon I get a phone call from Mark just as I've come in from the gym. There has been some emergency; the absence of any details—he is too rushed to fill me in for now—frightens me. Is Wally OK? I say. Yes, Wally is OK. But there is some medical appointment that possibly involves a hospital stay in Boston. And could I take Arden to the kennel?

Arden has been to the kennel many times before—it is said that he feels at home there—so of course. There is no problem getting him into the front seat of the car. He seems perfectly content, a gentleman in the passenger's seat, looking out at the pine trees and the Christian motel and the occasional gas station. But his head looks left as soon as I turn onto Nauset Road: maybe he already smells the poop, the obedience, the fear. Still, he keeps his chivalrous posture. He has too much dignity to whimper or whine. I park, open my door, open his door in order to hook the leash onto his leather collar. He will not move; even when I try to pick him up by the haunches he will not move. He has willed himself to weigh ten cinder blocks. He wants me to get the message. He has put up with enough, enough change, enough with being a good boy, dammit. He is middle-aged. And now he is losing his human, whom he's been watching out for ever since he was taken into the house, and his devotion isn't even enough to keep him well, to keep him in the world. It will take two people from the kennel to get him out of the car, and when he does move finally, he trots with ease, as if to shame me in front of these strangers, as if to say, Oh, Paul, what was all the fuss about?

Heroes

No die-ins except a brief one at the Outer Cape to force the Massachusetts Department of Public Health to agree to a treatment preventing pneumonia. It's a different AIDS world here versus the city world, where, as part of ACT UP and TAG, men and women demonstrate, call out, and confront, and get what they need from those in power, make sure drug approvals speed up through a bureaucracy that has brutality and murder in its DNA. It's not that anyone is any less energetic about saving lives at the end of the world. In fact, many have spent their time on the front lines before their arrival here. It's just that in a town that comports itself as a haven, where there's no resistance from within, the desire to save lives takes a different shape. It happens in houses, behind blinds pulled down, and you don't always know who the heroes are. The situation's far too grave for anything but the immediate. And who's certain if they're really helping when the terms of the illness shift from person to person? Heroes: They might not even want other people to know whom they lifted from the shower stall or off the floor. And they probably hate the neatness of the word.

Mother

What has happened to my mother? It isn't enough to say she's gotten older. All people, if they're lucky, get older. Skin sags, hands mottle, eyes and brows lighten as if bleached from within, but some people are still themselves. Some keep their energy, their sense of humor, their charisma. I hold the photo she sends me in my hand. My brothers and I blame our father for exhausting her, but I wonder how much of this exhausting she's done to herself. I slide out a photo album from underneath my bed. Here she is, in the earliest picture I have of her, by the ocean in Beach Haven, smiling with so much electricity, it is hard to take my eyes off her. The wide mouth, the hazel-brown eyes, her brows, thicker than you'd expect on a young woman: her beauty is more than the sum of her features. There's a quality in her that's elusive and complex, and that quality overpowers everyone else in her group, including her mother and friend Rita. But now she carries herself with a caution that suggests she never knew what it was like to attract others, both women and men. Maybe this is how a culture kills you, not through isolation or boredom or soul-impoverishing distraction, but by telling you that beauty is trouble. By telling you that maintaining your appearance is vain. By telling you that too much self is sex—and that sex is a threat to the status quo.

What must it be like for my mother to see me reaching toward another life? Every time she took a step toward another life? Well, maybe that step took her to a bad place. Maybe if you're not fully alive it isn't so hard to die. It is like going into an all-consuming corporate job and not considering the costs to yourself. You can convince yourself you are doing good by it. You say it's for the sake of your family when in fact you're just giving yourself up to the Big Greedy Force that has always been waiting to eat you up. Not quite death with a capital *D*, but another version of it. Capital *D* in disguise, making your acquaintance from an early age so you can get dressed for him, wait for him to point you to the room where you will sleep for the night, and the next night.

Once, in an unguarded moment, she tells me, "Your father wasn't my first. He doesn't know that." I don't really know what to do with the news. I feel honored, and somewhat startled to carry it, hold it close. Who wants to be the bearer of another secret, which has its costs? It is both a confession and an admission of pride. I had another life—*other lives*—before your father broke me. I can feel her testing my reaction. But I don't know why she's telling it to me. Why must my mother break some boundary whenever she wants to feel intimacy?

I tear into the harness, which is already several sizes too small. The harness that has been in use through many generations, on both sides of the family, its hide cut from early Catholicism, not enough money, class aspiration, learned passivity, practicality, family catastrophe. By tearing into it, I challenge and threaten everyone else who says no, no, no, no, no to themselves. That doesn't mean I don't feel shame and regret. Throwing off that harness is like coming out. It doesn't happen just once, the way they say it does in the literature of identity politics. No, I do it every day of my life. The practice keeps me alert, awake. And it still manages to chafe my skin red.

Musicale 2

Billy is too sure of himself, of his jokes. Or it could be that the reception of his performance is beyond concern at this point. It's the second Café Musicale, one year after the first, and in the interim it's become a legend. Billy presides over the Common Room as if it's his living room, certain, but maybe too certain, that he is loved by us. He doesn't seem to apprehend whether we get his inside jokes or not. He doesn't see that some wince when he starts in on his imitations, embarrassing imitations, of the people closest to him, some of whom are sitting in the front row. There's nervousness in the air, stale. People tap their feet, shift, cough, yawn, scratch their ears, rub their nostrils, adjust their posture in their chairs. Faces are frozen with smiles of support, eyes emptied of inner feeling. Some look out the window in the hope a storm could shut the whole night down. There's still definite love for Billy, but it's a challenge to love someone who is fucking up to the point where he is not noticing the reactions of his audience. The night is in service of a cause, but Billy has inadvertently turned the evening into a celebration of him, or at least his circle of accomplished friends. For a minute he seems to have forgotten that people are suffering and dying, including some people in this room. If only we were able to admit to ourselves that Billy, too, is on the way to dying, we might have real compassion.

Painters show slides. Poets read poems written especially for the night. Fiction writers read excerpts from novels in progress. The performances are just as animated as last year's musicale, if determinedly more so, but they're overshadowed by Billy's elaborate commentaries, which sometimes go on for minutes. We are waiting for logs to catch fire and flare. Billy is speaking in fondness and admiration, but his interpretations are twisted, broken by non sequiturs. He makes us all extensions of him, we're his minions. Here I'd thought he was our biggest fan and now it turns out he contains multitudes.

But perhaps a more morbid story is at work here, and it's taken me this long to see: Is Billy losing it? Is his breakdown happening right in front of our eyes? Maybe his verbal wandering is simply the first sign of dementia and we're all gathered inside the edge of the world. And we can't walk out, the way one might want to walk out of a John Cassavetes film when Mabel's disintegration at the dinner table might be too much to take. We're hostages of a film, of one another, this illness, this chaos.

At intermission, I walk up to Polly. "They shoot horses, don't they?" she says, referring to another director's film. And neither of us smiles. The joke isn't easy to make as she loves Billy, loves him as she would her brother.

When it's my turn to read, a mysterious, unexpected anger surges through me. I can't seem to find the voice that would transform the material, transform this night. What could one read to lift this evening? There can be something enthralling about any performance that comes so near to unraveling, when the performer misreads the audience, alienates them with his self-involvement, then somehow brings them back, and the audience is so grateful to be taken back, taken home, riveted all the more for being ferried from danger to safety. But I am not that kind of clown, or hero. The voice in me just wants to get through the performance, through this night before things get any darker, meaner. I read a little too fast. Human aspiration is being crushed—or is it love? Care feels like a vain project tonight, impossible in the face of outsize forces. Last year's inspiration haunts this year's disaster, and how could we not be furious at God for making a disaster of the night? Why does God let this happen to Billy in front of all the people who love him best?

God's Silence

The churches in Town turn their backs on the sick in Town, but that is not why I've turned my back on God. The churches' failure is not news: even the ACT UP protesters throwing communion hosts on the floor at mass has ceased to shock after five years. Nothing I've known about the world feels permeable anymore, and the surfaces it gives back—trees, water, the sky—feel as hard and opaque as the bottom of a frying pan. In Ingmar Bergman's *Winter Light*, the priest tells a congregant that he couldn't reconcile his loving God with the atrocities being committed in the Spanish Civil War, so he ignored the atrocities. It makes more sense to deny God's existence, he says, because the brutality of man needs no explanation. But what about God's brutality? says the man. Later in the film, another congregant wonders about the church's fixation on Jesus's suffering. What about all the betrayals he bore? he asks. Wasn't God's silence worse? The priest answers yes, and wonders whether to hold a service when it's clear that people haven't bothered to fill the pews. He decides to do it anyway, and the bells ring and ring and ring.

19

The Smallest Apartment in the World

My new apartment is the smallest apartment in the world, about six by six, just enough for a narrow bed along the window, a desk with shelves above it on the opposite side. There is a tiny bathroom and a strip of kitchen, with a toy-sized refrigerator-freezer. Blue indoor-outdoor carpet that gives off a faint hint of mildew. An outside staircase blocks the front window, but beyond that I see the Town beach and full harbor, boats of all sizes, MacMillan Wharf, the bluffs of Truro, and Long Point Light. John Dowd, the painter, lives across the hall in a space a bit bigger than mine. Some nights I hear piano playing, people singing around the piano, and I go over sometimes to join them, but not often, as I am shy. Lately my old shy self, the earliest self I knew, has come back to meet me.

Maybe that's why I like the fact that the apartment is high above Town, high above the funky beach out back. It's part of a building owned by Madelyn Carney, another painter in Town. Generations of Provincetown artists and writers have put in their time in this house, and I like joining their company. It is removed from the clamor of the street. I can almost afford it through the summer, and through the next winter, when the rent goes by a different schedule. It's more affordable, and I can pay by the month rather than for the entire season.

My friends call it 411, as that's the address of the building.

After paying my summer rent, I have only a hundred dollars in the bank. Many people get by with only a hundred dollars in the bank, but for me it is psychologically treacherous. I suspect this comes from having grown up with a father who never took toll roads in order to save twenty-five cents. Not that he didn't have money—he had plenty of money, all of which he put into stocks and CDs and IRAs. Only that the possibility of losing it was always on his mind, from how much toothpaste he allowed himself to squeeze on his brush to making sure he ate everything on his plate when he went to a buffet restaurant. As a result I have lived a life not caring about money, which is another way to say I've remained a child. But such choices indicate I'm just as scared of losing money as my father. We just have opposite responses to the possibilities of crisis.

There was a tough month over the past winter when Lucy and I went to the Lighthouse, a restaurant in Wellfleet, one day. It was during one of those stretches when the rain was ongoing, like in Ireland or Iceland, the climate of one of those northern countries where the nights are too long. The trees across the street were heavy and wet, a dazzling spring green. Another winter that wouldn't let go. Lucy still had plenty of money from her advance and offered to lend me some. My chest swung open, my pulse slowing down inside my wrists and neck. This touched me. Then weirder feelings rushed in: Would Lucy expect a deeper commitment from me? Would this change our friendship, the weather of it? Would I always be indebted to her, in some way, even when I paid her back? So I said no, but thanked her profusely, my scalp warm from the radiator at my back.

The strange moment continues. I am not poor the way genuine poor people are poor—I need to admit that to myself. There is always someone to invite me over to dinner, and I am definitely not yet stealing boxes of pasta from the A&P. Maybe I am just trying to hasten disaster imaginatively so that if it happens I'll be prepared. But to be in this position is to disrespect my father: all the sacrifices he made to make sure he and his loved ones would never feel the sting of poverty ever again. It is to fail his vision for himself somehow. All those years of music lessons, musical instruments, the encouragement, the faith that my brothers and I could be extraordinary creatures if we simply worked hard enough.

Then I make a mistake. I admit to my parents I'm finding it hard to pay my car insurance, other bills. Instantly my candor is transmuted in their minds as a tale of woe in which I am selling my butt on the street. Maybe they picture me moving in with a man who will use me, take everything he wants from me, then cast me off, like the hustler Alex in *Dawn: Portrait of a Teenage Runaway*, an

ABC Movie of the Week from my youth, another warning film, which managed only to make squalor seem satisfying and electric.

One day a letter arrives from my father. I keep it beneath a pile of junk mail, think I might not ever open it—or at least today. But curiosity gets the better of me. Am I surprised? He wants me to come home to Florida. The request, the audacity, the demand behind the request is a shock—I'm asked to choose between loyalty to my family and independence. He makes several appeals to my self-esteem, as if to say the life I've chosen is antithetical to my ideals. I can tell how much effort he's put into these paragraphs. He's given this some work. My father is brilliant in the department of math, but as far as putting words to the page? He's refused to nurture that side of his brain. He should have given me the letter to edit before mailing it to me, just the way he used to give me rough drafts when he was president of the Anchorage Point Civic Association or chairman of the Cherry Hill Planning Board. I could have said, The logic in this sentence is faulty. I could have said, The comparison in paragraph two is sentimental. I feel his frustration with every sentence, as if composing it got in the way of all the other tasks he'd bulleted on his to-do list: spreading fertilizer on the backyard, installing sprinkler system pipes in the front to keep the date palm green. The raw need is so palpable that I stare at the final paragraph frozen, unable to move for an hour. I hear a few stray notes from John Dowd's piano, then silence, deep winter silence. Trees creak outside. The mere act of reading the letter feels like it's bringing hurt to my father, to my mother, to me. All our loneliness, our need to be simultaneously together and apart.

Maybe this plea involves a generalized fear of sex, my sex, camouflaged by the fear of AIDS. But what if this request isn't even about me? If I go down to Florida, maybe he is then off the hook for spending time with my mother. He can remain in his own separate world, back in New Jersey. What does he do in his own private Idaho? Does he miss us; our dog, Pebbles; going out to dinner and running into random neighbors? Or is it a relief to be away from all that pressure, that expectation, social or self-imposed? Always somebody tapping you on the shoulder, always someone suggesting you didn't do that job right—see the mistake in that equation? That sloppiness? Maybe it feels like he's back at work, and he hasn't yet shaken off those feelings, even though he's been retired for a few years.

But do I respond to the letter? I wonder if it would hurt less to write back to him, but I don't. Why? Maybe because I know he still has the power to convince me out of here.

Sleep Tight

Polly calls one night, in the middle of the night, hours after I've gone to sleep. She asks if she can stay at my place: she and Richard are fighting, terribly, but she doesn't want to talk about it, can't talk about it yet. Her voice sounds stoic; she isn't crying. I tell her I don't know where she's going to sleep, but she says she'll sleep on the floor, on the carpet; she'll bring some blankets and sheets, and she'll borrow a pillow of mine, is that OK?

What will happen if I lose my favorite couple, the couple who affectionately call me their gay boyfriend? I shouldn't make this about myself, but they are my sturdiest connection to the straight world, the world of my upbringing, though they're both more queer than any other straight person I know. I don't ask any questions when Polly knocks at the storm door that never quite shuts or fits. The night is too charged, bleak; it's written in her eyes and in the corners of her mouth: she looks hunted. I will not ask of her, or impose on her, or even expect her to hug me: I see those notes in her face. She makes up a nest by the east-facing window, perpendicular to the bed. The apartment is a treehouse. There are ghosts outside on the tips of the dune grass. Sleep is the means by which we take ourselves out of adult terrors and back to childhood, where we'd never expect to lose anyone.

Library

Elizabeth comes over one day, sits on my bed, and dozens of copies of *Honcho*, the magazine, spill out onto the floor beneath the mattress. It is an archive, a multitude, a veritable Niagara Falls all over again. I had no idea I'd been buying so many; they must date back to October 1991, when I first arrived in Town, not a single month missed. Elizabeth's laugh is so loud, I'm sure it passes through the floors and walls of 411. But it isn't the laughter of shaming. I'm sure it's about the look on my face, which might be pulled into so many directions my eyes must pop. When my mother found my stash at home, she couldn't resist making me feel filthy, as if she'd pored over every image, every page herself, and hated it all the more because she found it sexy, hated what it made her.

Boatyard

It's always daunting to slip down the street to the Boatyard, even in the middle of the night. Someone could be walking by, usually it's a group, laughter brought on by too much booze. But what if it's someone I have a routine casual banter with, say, the lady in the health food store, the guy who signs me in at the gym? All sorts of people call themselves sex positive, but they might think differently of me if they saw me rushing down that notorious lane, hands in my pockets, steeling my shoulders, as if I'd just shoplifted a pork chop and held it under my arm. Guess who I saw going to the Dick Dock? that person might say. And the unspoken shared belief involves stereotypes of unmanageability, trashiness, self-disgust, disease sharing, and a pitiful sense of: Couldn't he do better? They'd never see me the same way again.

Even in a sex-positive church, sluts are not always viewed as high priests.

Of course once I'm walking among the boat hulls, I feel uncannily safe, even if I could possibly trip on an iron spike, conk my head against a low beam. Though it's all in the dark, it's all pretty easygoing and respectful, with bursts of group intensity. The sex I see is what's called safe sex: blow jobs and hand jobs. If horniness weren't narrowing my perception, I'd be able to step back and see how cinematic it is. All these bodies moving—it is like a scene out of Fellini if Fellini had been queer. No wonder the moon likes it here, shining a trail on the harbor from the Truro bluffs right to this very spot. There's a swarthy, muscular bull, with the face and demeanor of a bouncer. He's reportedly a famous nightclub promoter. People from every corner of life show up here. I've tried to catch his eye all summer, but it's been hopeless. I've even given up on looking at him when I pass him on the sidewalk, if only out of self-respect—I don't want to think of myself as a creep, the kind of person who *leers*. I'm not his type, clearly. I don't have big enough muscles, don't have big enough attitude. My swagger would never match his, which was probably cultivated by his relatives on the streets of Napoli, then Bensonhurst. Possibly he wants someone with classic features, more all-American, the polar opposite of him. But in the dark he's a different human. His eyes practically tear up when I touch his neck. I crouch down to suck his dick but he really wants to suck mine, and I back into a post and concentrate on his mouth. I close my eyes. I'm as happy as if I've published a book.

Nameless

Stranger whose name I'll never know, under the pier, in the darkness. What luck to be here with you. To hold parts of you in my mouth. To be held by you, to kneel down in the sand with you. To stand up again. To press my mouth to yours with a little pressure, then more until it almost hurts: teeth to teeth. To press my thumbs against the expanse of your forehead. To let you know your head—and the skull beneath it—is beautiful to me.

To know we don't have a history. No names to exchange and no obligation.

And the almost joy in letting you go.

20

The Hours

It's been months since Hollis and I have spent any time together. The unraveling—any other word seems too extreme—doesn't seem to have been marked by any incident. If anything, it feels like we've gotten too close. Playing around that way can be dangerous, especially when the chemistry (our ability to crack up at each other's jokes) is undeniable. Does it make him sad? My sadness and confusion have been so pervasive I'm not even sure I can feel them as such. To say we lost something would be to say there was actually something valuable between us, something to lose. But hope was never attached to our afternoons. Maybe it's too much to call them afternoons—*hours*. Let's just call it as it is.

We are seated outside Café Express, in the cluster of cedar-shake buildings across from the post office. We have just worked out. Everyone in Town comes here, which means I'm always running into someone, there's always a hug, an ebullient hello, but nothing goes unrecorded: faces, gestures, stray words. Hollis isn't talking much today. Deep down, in a place I don't care to inhabit, I am on fire; I am furious with him for disregarding the possibility of us as worthy of examination. I have ceded all the power to him, it's my own fucking fault. It's hard to find my feelings. Hard to see feelings as important when we are living in the middle of so much death. Not long ago, Jaco, his ex, took a turn for the worse, healthwise. And maybe that explains Hollis's resistance to tearing up his life once more? He couldn't build a new life without tearing up the last one. He'd have to say those experiences didn't count.

In spite of all this, Hollis still wants to be my friend. He still wants to go food shopping together, still wants to drive up Cape, or up to Boston. He agrees to drive me to the oral surgeon in Hyannis to get a wisdom tooth extracted, to take me home when I'm still in the haze of general anesthesia, sticky, warm cotton jammed in the corner of my mouth—an hour drive there and back when he had a thousand things due: no small favor. Once we got back to Town, I didn't even know I'd walked right past Norman Mailer, in the tiniest possible bikini no less, until it was pointed out to me.

One evening Hollis tells me he is setting me up with someone. The someone turns out to be a lovely guy, smart and sexy, with an inquisitive face and a dark, dashing, foppish curl atop his high forehead, but he's someone I couldn't possibly be drawn to because he isn't—isn't, well—*Hollis*! I try my very best to cooperate with this plan but I just can't. On our second date, in the middle of sex, he leans into me, bites my ear to tell me that he loves me. I freeze into my back teeth, as if my mouth's been stuffed with cold rice. I'm too upset to say, You do not. I bet you don't even know my middle name, dammit. You could have at least waited until the fifth date.

Expedient
But I get why he wants to get together *right now*. There isn't much time for any of us. What else do you do when the world is ending?

Adam & Steve
Every two months I see them, two devoted older men who look like tiny versions of Popeye. I imagine they've been here since the 1930s, when Portuguese women, open-minded and cosmopolitan, rented rooms to men. They wear cardigans and shorts in all kinds of weather and white knee socks that conjure up lederhosen. They live in a cedar-shake house surrounded by a chain-link fence almost as tall as they are. They've been a couple so long they don't even know when they started to resemble each other. Possibly they've been together since the beginning of time, and their union precedes all other unions, heterosexual and homosexual, and they are the true parents of us all. Adam and Steve, in the words of a tired joke. One of them is said to host a show featuring the music of John Philip Sousa on WOMR, the local radio station. It is very possible they have the best sex in Town, taking each other's loads

night after night, and why shouldn't they? It wouldn't even occur to them to worry about AIDS. They were together before that.

Refusal

This refusal to get tested: is it murdering me? Maybe *refusal* is too strong a word—*refusal* suggests agency and resistance, and my own position? Well, it's not even a position. It's procrastination, plain and simple, like my father not getting to the second item on his to-do list for a dozen years. But even that isn't cowardice, and I'm feeling cowardly, while at the same time I know I'm brave, very brave. Just for waking up. Just for meeting my friends day after day. There are all kinds of suicide, and maybe I'm just doing a long, slow suicide, another version of what my mother is doing to herself. What are the costs to the brain, the heart, the lungs, the skin? The hair is already receding from around my temples. And I'm not simply talking about disease as if it were lying in wait in me. I'm talking about holding the wave of dread back five times a day. Trying to silence the howl of illness.

21

Lonely People

Goofy bright eyes that want to laugh, muscular calves, Caesar haircut—he's been around Town for some weeks, and it's been impossible not to take him in. I've heard bits of his voice, one that's hard to describe. It slides between a low register and high, without warning. He does not do *th*'s at the ends of words—*youth* becomes *yoot*. English is his language, but he speaks English as someone who is also proficient in another language. It sounds like he's disciplined it out of his expression. Is he Lebanese? Greek? French Canadian? Israeli? I cannot pin him down. Sometimes he is in leather, sometimes he is in drag. He defies compartmentalization, and that's what says *magnetizing* to me. Up against him, everyone else looks like they're cramming themselves into framed boxes just so others will know how to interpret them: top, bottom, butch, queen, geek, party boy. He is all of the above at once: simultaneity incarnate.

One day, biking down Shank Painter Road, I catch him smiling at me beside the entrance to the A&P parking lot. He's on a bike, too, and if I were bolder I'd stop to say hello, instead of driving forward on Shank Painter, past the damn A&P, when I actually came out here for just that purpose. I'm long past saying to myself, What is wrong with me? And instead I remember seeing him dancing the other night, up on the go-go box at the Crown and Anchor's Back Room. He is a part of Ryan Landry's House of Superstar, a dance party that happens once a week, the same party that Hollis's Lou dances for. Queer people and straight people dance side by side at these parties—that doesn't mean the parties feel neutered or well behaved. The dancing is enthusiastic, it never lags. People are always out on the floor. Out in the middle of the floor a demure white girl mock-buttfucks some huge Puerto Rican guy with huge forearms, his mouth wide open in comic agony and loving every minute of it. The whole night has quote marks around it, but the quotes are as much playful as they are nihilistic. One night an oversize replica of an AZT capsule hangs from the ceiling. It glitters in the smoky air, blue band around the center, while people dance around it, fully aware that the drug that's supposed to be extending their lives is poison, is only making them sicker—and some corporation out there is accumulating a lot of wealth.

The DJ doesn't let a night go by without spinning "Lonely People," though its actual title is longer than that. At the beginning of the song there's an exchange between a prospective club-goer and a bouncer. To the clubgoer, who's certain she's on some guest list, the bouncer says, *There is no guest list tonight.* Though it's all a joke, the bouncer's voice burns, as the scenario takes place outside a club, in front of others. The clubgoer's presumed entitlement: well, you're indicted, too, because you know that desire to be a part of, to be included. At the same time you know the point of such an evening is to be inclusive, democratic, to take on people at all levels, no matter the race, gender, economic position, or sexual category.

And the paradox is there, always there, never corrected. For such a night to work it needs to be fueled by those opposing energies. To be cool, which is by its nature exclusive. And to be open enough to let everyone in.

One Wednesday, after he comes down from the go-go box, the man from Shank Painter Road walks right up to me, smiles, asks me what I like to drink, and offers to buy one for me. He puts his hand on my chest, then on my face. It is a public gesture, and it kills me, and I like it very much, possibly too much. He is claiming me and wants other people to see it. He is conferring power in an arena in which power has nothing to do with money. Power is more allur-ing, and maybe scarier, when its currency has nothing to do with money. How do I measure it?

It takes him a while to come into focus, and maybe I'm drawn to that quality about him, as Hollis was nothing but focus from the get-go. There is someone new to learn about the man I'll call Noah.

Lying together in bed the next morning, I find out he was a law-yer in Montreal before he came to Provincetown. He was in a long relationship with another man. He broke up with him, then went with a new boyfriend to India, where he traveled all over, from Goa to isolated mountain towns, before moving on to Bali. This might be why he carries the characters of so many parts of the world with him. He is single now, newly single, at least after some months. Too much sun floods my eyes, and I burrow my face into his back just to keep the dark in. I love the way *lawyer turned go-go boy* sounds when I say it to myself or when I imagine saying it to Polly.

We have a lot to talk about: so many people we have in common in Provincetown and downtown New York and Boston. And he loves books. He has deep opinions about books. He says he likes books with sentences that are long and difficult to write and read, Proustian sentences, those designed only to be read rather than spoken. Is this a French thing? He professes to a love of construction, artifice, which makes sense given his interests in leather and drag, but he doesn't describe it as such. That would be pretentious, too knowing. I'm not exactly sure I share his appreciation of the long sentence. I appreciate long sentences, but I don't want to be in a world in which everyone wears the same outfit around the table: What about Mary Robison? My hero, Joy Williams? Jane Bowles?

In no time at all I'm in love with Noah. And I don't receive his love as a demand, or something I don't deserve. Occasionally he reminds me that he is not a US citizen, and at any moment, in the night or in the morning, he could be pulled out of bed, along with all the other Canadian citizens in Town, as part of some sweep. His story strikes me as abstract, but I'm still scared of the possibility of an ending. It smokes up the atmosphere of every room we're in, and gives an on-the-spotness to our situation, which can be exciting, but it can also keep the two of us in line. Does he want to keep me in line? By bringing it up, he tells me not to expect too much of us. Maybe the devotion in my face, in the way I kiss and hold him, needs correcting. Just a splash of cold water. I get it.

He works as a houseboy at the Manchester Inn, a guesthouse with a slutty reputation. I'm not sure it's sluttier than any other operation in Town, but the place sells sex, a big hot tub in the backyard, a clothing-optional policy, though I've never seen anyone walking around naked. Along with the other houseboy (whom I have a small crush on; he could pass for a curly-haired straight boy from Scituate), he sleeps up in the eaves of the house in what amounts to a bunk bed. It is a ship up there, cozy, especially when it is cold and windy out. And yet there's something unkind about it, something uncomfortably like, what—a storage unit? Raw lumber, bare light bulbs, no pretense that the owner tries to make it livable or aesthetic. But that seems to be an aspect of the pact you sign: nothing matters more than sex and that is what you're working for. The owner, a man named Paul, has a wry booziness about him, but he's always friendly to me, and I've never seen him be anything but friendly to Noah. He seems to be far less interested in making money than he is in maintaining the inn's louche appeal. He wants it to be a bit sleazy, wants to make sure that hot guys, as well as once-hot guys who have gone to seed, fill that hot tub. The two houseboys make many jokes about that hot tub, and swear they'd never put a bare foot in it despite all the liquid shock that goes into it on a daily basis. There are enough chemicals in that cauldron to burn the paint off the bottom of a boat. Or to cure AIDS, for that matter. Jokes are made about leading the sick in Town to the hot tub so they can be cured, the lesions closing up on their skin, their T cell counts shooting as high as the roof.

As much as Noah is compelled and entertained by this raunchy atmosphere, he pretty much knows he doesn't want to sleep there. Noah will sleep on the beach in Bali, Noah will shit in a pail in India, but he will not sleep in the attic of the Manchester Inn. So Noah and I take to the twin bed in the smallest apartment in the world, one of us smashed up against the windowsill. It's a relief to sleep so close after I've kept a space open for someone beside me, even when I slept by myself.

Sometimes at night I lie awake wondering what Hollis is thinking. He seems expectedly cheerful when I run into him at the gym, and he knows Noah, professes to like Noah, even when I probably mention his name too much. I'm not being careful enough to keep myself in check. I suppose I am happier than I've been in a long time, even if I haven't been spending very much time with Hollis. I probably don't do a very good job of spreading my devotion around—I just don't know how. When I care about someone, it is impossible for that person not to know it. And when my head turns away? Well, I am somewhat like a pit bull, tethered only to the person on the other end of the leash.

I suspect that's my mother's influence. How to be anything to anyone if not another twin?

Perhaps this is why Hollis is furious with me one day. We're sitting outside our old haunt, Café Express, and the sun is hard and bright on his face. His outburst is very much out of the blue, no buildup, no signs. He claims that I've pulled back from him. And maybe that's true, but I haven't abandoned him in my inner life— will I ever? I try my best to listen to him, shifting in the patio chair, looking down at the tuna sandwich and chips on my plate, which have now lost all semblance of taste. I break up a potato chip and don't eat it. Somebody bikes by repeatedly ringing a bell, though no one is blocking his path. I'm shocked, so angry that this fucker would have the gall to be mad at me. What between us has ever nurtured this rough feeling? He's never owned me.

I don't get angry back at Hollis, which likely only increases his fury. He should be happy—my detachment, my "good-natured self-control," as Joni Mitchell would sing it, was taught entirely by him. Or at least he drew it out, gave it a shape. Shouldn't he be proud of me for that? Haven't I been a successful student of the heart? He shouldn't be shocked. Any queer man has learned how to keep his feelings in check better than anyone else. From our earliest age, we've learned not to look the sexiest guy in the room straight in the eye. We've made sure to temper our excitement lest the sexiest guy shake his head in disgust, or rally the others around him to laugh at us. We've never unlearned what we knew. We still do it today, in certain places (say public restrooms) and certain parts of the world (say Alabama, say non-urban Florida, say portions of Philadelphia), even though it makes us cringe to admit it to ourselves. Even if we dress like bros or frat boys. Even if we think of ourselves as men above fear: people who couldn't give a shit about others' reactions: see our expressive gestures and voices, our eye rolls. Whatever the case, we know what it involves to fit in and thus ghost away the inner life. To kill the spirit out of ourselves.

As to what that might do to our psyche and soul? As to how that might punish away our ability to love someone over time?

Welcome to homophobia.

Pee

Noah bikes ahead of me on the way to Herring Cove. I don't mind that he's biking so fast, but I wish he'd look over his shoulder to see if I'm still behind him—just once? What if I got caught behind a truck? We lock our bikes to the split rail, walk through the woods, walk out onto open marsh, where we slosh through tidal pools as warm as Miami water. The sun is hot out here, the minnows are active around our feet, and by the time we're out on the beach, we need to get in the bay to cool off. We step in an inch at a time, arms clenched, faces tense, tightening, grimacing, our *balls*—probably better just to plunge into any New England ocean. "This isn't Goa," Noah cries. But before long, eyes relax, we're not pulling air into our lungs through our teeth. We walk closer to the shoreline, root ourselves into sand. Noah hugs me from behind, holds me in place. It's good to have this afternoon together, so good we managed to make our frenetic schedules mesh. I'm leaning back into him when I feel something warm, warm water. The tropics are here. Noah is laughing. He's peeing on me. "You can't pee on me in public," I cry. "Look, there are people out there." "Oh yes I can," he says, "I can, I can, I can," and I try to wrench away and we're both cracking up.

Smooth

Noah's body is impossibly smooth, no hair anywhere but on his head. In a day or two he'll feel scratchy: five o'clock shadow but not on the face, and he'll itch, or feel the prospect of a rash coming on, and he'll shave all over again, and I'll do it along with him. We'll convince ourselves this is sexy, because in a time of barriers, skin-to-skin feels transgressive, feels close and alive. But this isn't just our idea: shaved bodies are all you see in porn. Body hair equals old, equals death, and who could blame any of us for wanting to turn ourselves into babies again? We hate old people because we're not going to be old. We deny age, abhor it, including any of the gay men who have made it to fifty, sixty, unscathed, whom we've declared are too timid and unadventurous ever to have been bottoms. Oh, not really. *God.* We just want to be in touch—or not out of it. There's so little to want that we have control of.

Signals

So many acquaintances of ours seem to want Noah when he's out dancing, up on the go-go box. They put their hands all over his legs and ass, and laugh, and Noah laughs, though a little nervously. I stand with my back to a pillar, watching casually, but trying not to watch too much: I don't want Noah to think I'm possessive. He'd be completely turned off by that. But that doesn't stop me from wanting to cry: Hands off. Are these guys even thinking about what Noah wants? Are they reading his signals? If a part of him does like the attention, they're not catching the anxiety, the hint of ambivalence in his eyes. That ambivalence is at odds with his tight, beaming smile. From my end, looking at those guys is as lousy as looking at drunken frat boys—and as boring. *Troubling.* Noah can take care of himself, but I know these guys wouldn't be touching him if they didn't think it gave them power and privilege. They're not doing it for anybody but some imagined ocean of others, out there in the dark, on the dance floor—or maybe for me. I know they don't like me.

Only one hour left until closing.

Wet

It takes a long time to get out of a latex shirt. His skin looks like it's been punished, like broiled flounder with diaper rash, though the rash isn't on his ass, but up through his lats. The baby powder he used before he put it on doesn't seem to have kept him dry. I help him squeeze out of the latex, the way I helped him get in. We laugh at the bald absurdity of the task: the unexpected tenderness of being this close, this intimate, this awkward, an act involving the body that has nothing to do with sex. Perhaps our laugh keeps it a little safe, keeps us from asking any questions: Why would you hurt yourself by putting on an impermeable man-made material that doesn't breathe? Is it even sexy, and for whom? Or is it just a figure for the probability of contamination, infection, taken to an extreme—a larger version of a condom?

I feel a little bit like a parent, my veterinarian grandfather, or some kind of midwife: I'm bringing Noah forth from the steaming, wet placenta back into the world.

22

Happy Birthday, Gay

I'm not working today, and I cannot even imagine having the focus or discipline to write. I wonder when my mother will call, and after I turn that over for a few minutes—it's 11 a.m., and where is she?—I decide to dial the number myself. Of course I know that part of that decision involves making her feel a little crappy for not calling me first thing.

"Honey, happy birthday," she says and her voice is unguarded and lovely, apologetic for not phoning me earlier—she had to stop at the store for dog food. Now I'm the one who feels crappy, because I'm talking to the mother I've almost forgotten, the sweet mother who doesn't obliterate me with excess wariness and concern. She's having a good day that sounds like it doesn't have very much to do with my day; she sounds so close, I can practically sense her across the room. Her smile, her bare arms, her tanned neck, crinkled, lightly sunburned above her coral-colored tank top. It's almost as if she's come back from the dead, but without any of that intensity or deep meaning. Is this what it is to feel safe? She'll be lost again to me, but for this minute I love her and feel it back, and it's the most supreme present for the day.

Noah has decided to invite a few friends over to his friend Lark's house. Lark and I have the same birthday, so Noah decides we'll spread it out between the two of us by sharing one elongated cake.

Walking up Tremont, I see bodies up ahead. Loud voices, a throng of young men filling up a tight yard lit by lanterns. And that's it: Lark's yard.

All these people! "Surprise!" I turn clockwise, lose my balance, shove my hands as far down into my pockets as I can. From their handsome, dazzled faces it's clear that this is *the* party in Town tonight. "Happy birthday!" the group roars, after Noah points to me. And then the chorus begins, and I startle, because I know not a single one. Everyone pretty much looks alike, from the same social sphere. None of the people I care about are here—and if they're here (Polly?) they're hiding, eager to leave, nothing in common with a scene, or with people drawn to socializing in A-list groups.

No one's relaxed, though they all pretend to be relaxed. Anxiety lifts and stirs the particles in the air. Two desires are happening at once: the need to hook up, and the work of naming and claiming social status—are you witty enough, sexy enough? And the latter desire always wins, canceling out the first because it's so much easier to solve.

In the '70s, two people would have probably cordoned themselves in the bathroom and blown each other hastily, then joined the big group again.

Noah comes up to me and hugs me in front of the crowd. I must feel it's my duty to say a public thing, or I'm called upon to do so. As I'm having a hard time getting my bearings, I probably thank everyone too eagerly, forgetting the fact that it's Lark's party too. I step backward, gesture toward Lark, who's sitting away from the lights, underneath the walnut tree on one of two banged-up Adirondack chairs. His eyes are characteristically wide, spiked with alarm, as it's his wont to scrutinize every voice, outfit, posture, and pair of shoes—the tool many a gay man has sharpened in order to feel on top of things, in social control. There's an acerbic look on his Scandinavian face. A blanket covering his knees, though it is a muggy summer night, and everyone around is in a T-shirt or tank top. He is thin to the point of translucence. He doesn't look like he feels so well, or is terribly interested in the rituals of celebrating another birthday. After the party resumes, I walk over to say hello, but he isn't interested in holding a conversation beyond hard pleasantries. Of all the people I know, Lark is the least likely to put on a good face, especially if he's not feeling well. And if I try to cheer him up a little, well—he'll make sure to say something a bit cutting. He'll say a word about the cut of my new shirt while pinching a bit of the fabric and rubbing it. He'll say aloud the name of a short story of mine that others have talked about and roll his eyes in exaggerated condescension, as if anything other than the work of staying alive is gross, pure vanity. I wonder what it would be like to address others by tossing verbal darts at them. Would life be thrilling, daring, subversive in a way I could never know? Would it free me to throw my notion of karma aside, to take up a stance that I believed I wouldn't count enough to hurt anyone?

Bitter queen, I think, relegating bitter queens to a time in the past, to the era of self-loathing, even though Lark and I are close to the same age. I'm allergic to bitter queens, even though I admire them, respect them, and know bitter queens are the truest rebels, rejecting all that is wrong about this world by pulling meanness into them and throwing it back out.

I move among the crowd, trying to find someone it would be easy to talk to, but I have only the social skills to make inside jokes about death and love, and these are the kinds of subjects that sag some people's faces, especially when they've had a lot to drink.

By midnight everyone is gone from the yard. Various groups lump and veer down the street, some toward the Crown, most to the A-House. "Thank you for the party," I say to Noah in a voice not much above a whisper. "That was really sweet of you to plan." Now that everyone's gone I can say it like I mean it. I didn't know till I said it aloud that I was afraid of sounding false.

I had no idea a birthday party would feel like the kind of work you should be paid by the hour for.

At my feet are tossed cups, beer bottles, tortilla chips moist from the cooling, humid air. "You're welcome," he says, but looks preoccupied, resentful. I think he'd been hoping he'd have a better time of it, and maybe I've been the obstacle to that better time. And now he's just exhausted.

Or maybe he realizes he just hosted a Gay Birthday Party, an event that fits exactly inside its category, and that was never his intention. Somehow his plans took on a life of their own.

We're never so far from the conventional, and that lesson grates into us.

23

House Music

Some of the great music of the era makes it to Provincetown, but much of it doesn't. Nirvana, Jeff Buckley, Liz Phair, Tori Amos, even Kate Bush's *The Sensual World*—I don't hear it lifting from the houses, or out at the gym. Maybe it's too tortured, but not tortured about the right things. It's not in sync with the hell going down here. The suffering in it might be too extreme, indulgent, artificial, though it believes it comes straight from the soul. It might not have enough wit and play in it. It edits out too much—black people, for one. When I ask my friend Pauline what she thinks of Jeff Buckley, and Pauline's opinion matters, as she runs MAP, my favorite clothing store in Town, she closes her eyes briefly, shakes her head no, without apology. And in her dismissal I know that that music isn't for us. Maybe that music knows about AIDS, or, later, Abner Louima, but it keeps those matters on the periphery, if it lets them in at all. Its problems aren't our problems. Its head is somewhere else, which means nonqueer white masculinity problems, and the utter tragedy of difficult women and/or not getting laid.

And yet the dreamy intensity of Jeff Buckley, the Led Zeppeliny hysteria of it, beautiful hysteria. I play it over and over, but listen with headphones, sneak it the way a young priest might sneak a look at one of the porn magazines underneath my bed.

The songs of Town are the songs of urban life: house music. It comes from African American, Puerto Rican clubs. Harlem, Flatbush, Washington Heights, Detroit, Chicago. Its roots aren't in the music of white people. Crystal Waters, Joi and Jorio, Digable Planets, A Tribe Called Quest. The songs are dreamy and smart and move with unexpected chord changes. They're never the anthems that make people clap at the edge of dance floors ("Rhythm is a Dancer," for example). These are the songs built for small spaces, DIY spaces, spaces the Giuliani administration will later discipline out of sight. The music doesn't contort itself to mass taste, maybe because there isn't much money to be made from such music. It's a labor of love, inevitable when you're just trying to keep each other alive. It has nuance, surprises in the bass line, or in the high vocals. It keeps rewarding you again and again, doing strange things to your body. You feel loose when you're dancing to it, perhaps because it makes you feel sexier than you are. There is rarely a single refrain. You'll never hear it in a Palo Alto Whole Foods fifteen years later; alas, it will disappear from playlists long before then. It's music for people who might already be high on certain kinds of drugs, but the drugs are warm and friendly enough. The Epidemic is present in every vocal line, even if devastating loss and chaos aren't the explicit subjects of the song. You can just feel it; you wouldn't be able to tame it out of those vocal leaps. It knows what true gravity is. Its purpose is to startle and reorient you through a set of tricks that will work its way into your psyche even if you don't know the musical terminology. Its work is about more than entertainment, though entertainment is never to be undervalued, diminished. Where else would joy come from? Where else would we find our joy?

SAs

Noah has a need to embarrass me as a way to challenge me. Sometimes this involves grabbing my hand and holding it as we walk through the streets of Boston's financial district, on a day trip. I want to hold his hand. I'm proud to be seen with him, connected to him, and I appreciate the way he pushes me out of my comfort zones, out of my frequent desire to recede, especially in a place like Boston, where queer couples should definitely be visible. We cannot forget our ACT UP principles, and besides, what living being, human or animal, is comfortable in the financial district of Boston, a city of liberal politics but conservative social mores? Queer, straight, black, brown, white. Dogs on the ends of leashes. Everyone walking around, wondering, Why am I outside myself, watching myself? Navigating through some pervasive cloud of fear, though no one calls it fear. In Town I'd gotten used to forgetting that particular fear, and now I'm dropped back to a former self, who cannot hide and must be accountable. It has the smell of a shirt I've forgotten to wash, and I simply want to wander away. Noah, on the other hand, appears to like fear; it is sex to him. It makes him animated and alert. It tells him he's feeling brave when he rarely gets to feel brave anymore. What a relief it is not to be one of these people walking by us, letting their routines bump them through the day, allowing those routines to keep them from being aware of the pain in others, the pain in themselves.

In the end, are we even noticed? Not really. No hate or contorted faces are aimed in our direction, but it does turn what was meant to be a casual day into the prospect of a showdown, a political action.

Sometimes I wonder whether Noah would be more comfortable visibly attached to someone who's more outrageous than he is. Today he's wearing a long necklace of green glass beads and cable-knit, cream-colored sweater pants that happen to show off the outline of his big, floppy dick. One day we will say genderqueer, but today there is no word, and people don't do so well with seeing when they don't have a category to help them out. It's like putting a frame around the world with a title and curator's description off to the bottom right—oh, now I get it. And who could be surprised that Noah's pet peeve is guys who call themselves straight-acting and -appearing, guys who think they're more achieved than others? Guys who want it both ways: straight white male entitlement while sucking cock behind closed doors. He calls the straight-acting and -appearing guys SAs, pronounced "sass," and speaks of them with such pain it's impossible to get to the bottom of his hurt.

Safari Club

On a different trip to Boston, I park on a street by the Flower Exchange, which might be a sketchy neighborhood, or maybe not—you never know how Boston changes block by block. I've just dropped Noah off at South Station, where he is bound for a train to Montreal. "I might not be let back in," he says, and by "in," he means into the United States, which only prompts me to hug him harder, in panic. Now I'm being buzzed into a sex club, but only after I promise, in writing, that I'm not a journalist, someone out to expose the place. The club has been on the city's radar, and there are multiple forces that want to shut it down, as those forces believe this is no era for a sex club, especially in the age of the Epidemic, but advocates of sex clubs state that people are most likely to have safer sex in controlled environments, where condoms are distributed freely. I can't imagine this place lasting much longer: how could it be making enough money to heat these cold and vacant halls? No one here, no surprise as it's the middle of the day, a frosty, low-lit afternoon when everyone is sitting at a desk in an office. But there's one guy around, a young, battered blond guy, with tattoos vining his arms, legs, chest, and back before anyone else has tattoos like that. It's a relief to stand in his minuscule room, to hold him in my arms from behind. For such a roughed-up guy, he's surprisingly sweet, a total gentleman. What would Noah say if he knew I was here? My gut feeling is that he'd probably think of it as a quick stop at Star Market to pick up corn on the cob and tomatoes. If only I could make him jealous. It's becoming clearer to the two of us that I care about sex more than he does. Sex for me is as essential as food, and he'd probably be relieved if I wasn't at him all the time, pressing my boner against the bottom of his spine. The guy swallows my load, and afterward my body freezes up in awe and dread. I don't even think I can walk. I'm not writing this as a confession.

Richard

At the gym, back in Provincetown, I'm always happy to see Hollis's old friend Richard, who's an appealing mixture of nihilistic, sweet, caustic, and very boyish. He likes to make me laugh. His is the most battered face I've ever seen, but he wears that batteredness beautifully, his earlier handsomeness still haunting his face. He comes from the East Village of Peter Hujar and David Wojnarowicz, and I wouldn't be surprised if he'd once interacted with those guys. Maybe had sex with them? His eyes are clear and bright to the point of being colorless, the most alive eyes I've ever seen on a person, as if he's spent years waiting for any human in his path to punch him. I don't know if his batteredness comes from years of heroin addiction, or from all the AIDS drugs he's had to take so far. It speaks from hidden pockets of air beside his back teeth. He has the aura of one of those people who would completely dismiss you if he didn't like you, didn't think you were worthy, so I'm always honored when he talks to me, which involves looking at me with the fullest attention, even though shyness crushes the words coming out of my mouth. Does he have a crush on me? Do I on him? Possibly—it's hard to see around feelings with the virus standing between us like an actual person. One day Hollis calls to tell me that Richard is in Beth Israel—do I want to drive up to Boston with Polly? "He has a high fever," Hollis says. "When are you leaving?" I say. "Oh, a half hour from now." I don't know why I don't drop what I'm doing and say immediately, Yes. Let me throw on a sweater. It isn't that I'm scared of seeing Richard die. I think our being there is only going to make something bad happen. It wouldn't be what Richard, who can't stand sentimentality, wants.

They go. I stay.

24

Vacation

We've decided not to dress like two queer guys from Provincetown—
no funny hats and no neobutch lumberjack wear—and as I drive toward the Saint-Armand border checkpoint, the stakes of that become
more immediate, less abstract. If the border patrol agent doesn't like
the way we look, he'll take us aside, and who knows if Noah will
ever be allowed back? Would I have to move to Canada and leave
Provincetown? A dozen cars idle ahead of us. My hands are cold, in
constant motion. To steady them I reach over for Noah's hand, and
he shakes me off, shakes his head like a disapproving teacher. That
disapproval is related to his collared shirt, which manages to take
away anything distinctive about his appearance. He's a lawyer once
again, but in weekend clothes. No one would ever be able to guess
that back on Cape Cod he was a person who had a special place in
his heart for rubber, latex, and leather.

When we answer the border patrol agent's questions, we answer
tersely, without any inflection or any eagerness to please. We're
performing what we believe he wants of men, especially two men
sharing one car. We tell him—*truthfully*—that we're here on vacation and fortunately he doesn't peer in and say, Do you have any
women hiding in there? His face is neutral. He hands back our passports without comment and we're on our way.

And now the trip can really begin. Now that we're into Quebec
adrenaline hits my bloodstream and I'm reading the surfaces
the way I'm used to reading the surfaces of Town—it is good to
have some new material to think into. I can say that its flatlands
look like the blueberry farms of South Jersey. I can say that the
houses with the mansard roofs and crisscross windows resemble
the "French Provincial" model homes in Huntshire, a subdivision
near where I grew up, in Cherry Hill. Noah tells me he never even
looked at those houses and finds my enthusiasms hilarious. He re-
peats the phrase "French Provincial," and laughs again. Of course.

I can tell he's relaxing too. He slides lower in his seat and tells me all about the old friends, a straight couple, we're staying with in the city this week.

Over the course of the next five days, I am in vigilant mode, like a deer beside a highway. I meet so many old friends and former business associates, I can't even remember their names. I want them to find me charming, winning, maybe because they're trying to pull those qualities out of me. These friends have all known Noah as part of Noah and Henry and I'm trying to measure up to his ex without even knowing Henry, who seemed for all intents and purposes a daddy, someone older and responsible, another lawyer. No one wants Noah to be different from the Noah they knew, even though he's left law and moved to Provincetown. I'd be so easy to blame if they found him judgmental or distant and didn't like his jokes. Didn't like the new person he was becoming.

I don't even have enough mental space to consider whether I like his friends. Like me, they like to laugh, even though it doesn't seem as if we have anything in common. None of them are in the arts, but I didn't expect them to be. Yes, it's a little lonely, but how could you be lonely when so many people are looking at you with benevolence, as if they'll continue to regard you and ask after you for the rest of their lives?

Or maybe it's just that I want Noah so much that the question of his friends isn't even relevant to me. It's made me a little blind, stupid to my needs, as happens when you might want someone who's always out of reach.

It doesn't help that I haven't spoken French since college, even though I love French, the sound of it, its tricky vowels, which feel elusive to the construction of my mouth, frustrating when I want to sound like a native speaker. I spend the better part of each conversation grabbing on to a few recognizable nouns and verb phrases and holding on. I nod a lot, laughing when I'm surrounded by laughter, hoping not to get caught.

All of which sounds like I'm not having a terribly good time. But I am having a good time, the best. I love Montreal, its style and panache, its resemblance to Europe, throwing the dowdy brick cities of the northeastern US into shadow. Rue Ste.-Catherine.

Diane Dufresne and her extravagant voice, her grandiose feathers. Pouding chômeur. Fries with mayonnaise. The hump of Mount Royal above the rooftops.

At night in his friends' guest room bed, I sleep as deeply as I've slept in years. I press my nose into the back of Noah's neck, holding on, possibly snoring. The work of pleasing is as hard as going back to law school, especially when I never imagined myself in front of a court.

On our final day we stop by Noah's parents' house. It's in a neighborhood where all the street names point to England rather than to France: Douglas, Bedford, Barclay, Rockland, Fleet. Noah has always made it clear that he grew up in English Montreal, and I'm meant to find that significant, even though I never fully grasp it. I park at the curb; we hang back a bit and look up at the house, a brick two-story that appears to have been built in the 1950s, more classic and restrained than the formidable Tudor next door. The neighborhood is posh, but subtly. It's a relief to know that I will be accepted, that Noah's parents have met boyfriends before, and we won't be met by incrimination and withholding.

That wouldn't happen with my mother and father, I think, with a pang of resentment, hurt. Maybe it's my fault—possibly I have been a *bad gay* by not finding boyfriends to take home to meet them. I have kept my gay life out of their sight when I should have been throwing boyfriends in their faces until they got used to them, until they got numb to them, cried, Enough already!

Noah's father welcomes us and ushers us inside. We sit on the sofa, where coffee is offered and poured by Noah's stepmother. As a unit everyone is cordial enough, but distractible too—the house operates through a culture of distraction and maybe that's why I don't take in faces, gestures, the pattern of the rugs, the view out the back window, or the style of furniture. Is it what we used to call colonial, a lot of maple? Do I not take anyone in because I'm reluctant to have an opinion, and to have an opinion is to judge? They're speaking English, but talking about a family matter I can't find my way into. I feel a little bit on the outside but it's a relief to be a spectator after I've been pulled close by his friends for days. I don't think I could say anything that would matter at all. I feel a little bit like I'm floating, nothing tethering me to the world of life and death. It's probably time to get back to my desk and pin myself to the earth with words. One more day now.

Noah needs to get something upstairs in his old room and I follow him up the steps. It's amazing to be in his childhood bedroom, and here I can feel the past of him, through the light falling through the window, falling on his dresser, the way a twin bed almost fills the snug space to capacity. I sit on the bed, pick up a polished black stone from the nightstand. And then his stepmother stands at the door. She isn't looking at Noah, or at any other object in the room, but at me. She does this out of Noah's sight. Instantly I know I have crossed a line that was never drawn, and never will be, just by sitting on his bed, just by suggesting—what? The fact that we share one, give each other blow jobs, and occasionally fuck? Her expression isn't theatrical, but it's scared and steady, as if she knows it isn't in her purview to tell me to stand up. I might as well have spilled bacteria in her house. I don't stand up, nor do I say, Is something the matter? The whole visit is sucked into the moment, into the scared look on her face. The quiet of it is so breathtaking I don't even discuss it with Noah now, or once we're driving south, away from Montreal.

It isn't until we've reached the checkpoint in Highgate Springs that we realize we've forgotten our preparations. We've forgotten to put on our blandest outfits, neglected to review the anticipated questions. Our reward? A border patrol agent who's on the young side, with a prow-like brow, whose face goes instantly hard the second he looks into the car. There's no doubt he'd offer us a different face if there were a woman in Noah's seat and a couple of kids coloring within the lines in the back.

I also suspect the name Provincetown, which shows up on my driver's license, must mean something to him.

He spends an obsessively long time scrutinizing our documents. When it seems he's done with mine he starts all over again, as if the printing on them has been altered or rubbed away. Cars keep moving through the stalls to the right and left of us. He asks us what we do for a living. "Lawyer," Noah says. "Clothing store associate," I say, cringing at the way it sounds. A few weeks ago Noah counseled me never to describe myself as a writer to border patrol because they always hate writers, think they're subversive. And that would only lead to more questions and his detainment at the border.

He also said border patrol can stop you if you avoid looking at the agent, or if you pay too much attention to him. The problem is I've taken this in so deeply that I squint and do a funny thing with my mouth and must stand out like an imbecile.

"What would a lawyer be doing with a store clerk?" As if he can't see we are boyfriends. He *knows* we are boyfriends, my God. He thinks he's giving the two of us a free pass, but he'll not give us that pass without pissing on us first.

We don't answer his question, but it's clear we were never expected to. He gives us back our passports and turns his head away.

"Can you believe that?" I say again and again over the next ten miles. "Welcome to America. I can't believe that motherfucker talked to us like that."

"Paul."

"I don't think I even want to live here anymore." And then I slam my fist down over my right knee for effect.

"Stop," he says, as if he's had enough and it's time for me to move on. The woods of Vermont are thick with birch and ash, and what is it I've lost?

There's a hill up ahead and I swerve into the climbing lane.

Violence doesn't always present itself in the form of a gun.

25

The New Yorker

Matt stands in the middle of the Work Center's parking lot one day, hungry to talk. He might be waving a piece of paper in the air. Even if he isn't, he's giving off the feeling that might summon that up: news of shock, news of heartbreaking happiness, news of life-about-to-change. He calls Elizabeth and me, the only people around, to tell us the *New Yorker* took one of his stories, a story he'd sent in the mail. It's a time when the *New Yorker* rarely publishes unsolicited fiction, and Elizabeth and I are so proud and thrilled, I almost forget I would have wanted that for myself once, not so long ago.

Elizabeth & Elvis

One night at a reading series in Town, Elizabeth reads from a new piece about Elvis. She speaks the whole narrative by heart, her eyes closed some of the time, her chin lifted at other times as if she is singing the words not just to the people in front of her but to the space above us, higher than the room. Her words are soft but not so soft we can't hear. Though the direct subject is the beauty of early Elvis's melancholy, it's also a piece about living amid so much loss, and how you can't count on very much if you're a broken old man at thirty-five.

Mirrorings

At another series, Lucy reads "Mirrorings," an essay about the liberation of childhood Halloween: to wear a mask is to throw off the shackles of a face. Multiple notes sound in the room. Disfigurement, drag, AIDS, the body in trouble. The room rings like a chord that goes on and on and on.

Shankpainter

Mindy gives us one of her photographs for the cover of *Shankpainter*, the Work Center's annual literary magazine, which a few of us are editing. It's a close-up of a woman's pubic hair, her fingers pressing into it. It's not an idealizing photo, or really all that erotic in the conventional sense. But it's not out to shock either; it says sex when forces in the culture say that sex is death. We think we've prepared ourselves for some possible flak—but we couldn't have predicted the half of it. Some Work Center administrators are not pleased, not pleased at all, especially given that they use the magazine for fundraising and grants. We are clueless Fellows, but to the Work Center's credit they don't ask me to change the image. The powers that be still print the issue and slide it into envelopes.

Ha!

Elizabeth and I are sitting in the jury room, around the table with the big writers, meaning those with several national awards. It's heated, but not unfriendly. Four fiction fellowships out of three hundred–plus applicants: how could the discussion not be heated, especially if people are doing this out of love for the Work Center, and no money? Elizabeth and I represent the two Second-Year Fellows involved every year, and as such it's hard work but an honor to sit in these seats. And yet we're all too aware of our position. Together we champion a particular manuscript, longer than usual, about an ongoing environmental emergency, which our fellow jurists dismiss, dislike, for what's called an overt political agenda. *Didactic*. Elizabeth and I feel chastened, miffed, but we refuse to give up our belief in the work. During the final meeting, an especially famous writer comes to weigh in after reading the semifinalists, and this time it's Grace Paley. Around the room we go to talk about the work in front of us. After discussing several applications, Grace gets to *the one*, looks at Elizabeth and me, pauses. She says, "This is an important story, this writer is writing important things." She says more, but that's all we take in. All disagreement comes to a stop in the room. The writer gets his fellowship, and

Elizabeth and I do not clap and gloat and do a little jig until we're outside in the parking lot.

Founders Club

Often Stanley Kunitz and Alan Dugan, the cofounders of the Work Center, show up at Fellows' events. They sit apart from the group, possibly expecting to be approached, but we're often shy as if they're the intimidating older relatives at a family gathering. Why? In truth, they're funny and eager to hold a conversation, but they must be approached. Elizabeth, for instance, gets along famously with Dugan, and I always end up talking to his wife, Judy Shahn, whose drawings I know from the pages of the *New Yorker*. But to talk with them upends our sense of collective identity. It's perhaps easier to think of ourselves as *emerging*—all of our best work still ahead of us—than it is to be in the club where we already have a body of painting or writing to which we have to be responsible.

If given the choice to be an adult or a child, most humans will choose the latter.

26

Koan

In the beginning of a relationship, sex starts in the kitchen, or maybe in the foyer, within sight of the neighbors if anyone chooses to look in. It might travel anywhere in the house, onto the stairs, into the shower. Sex has an energy all its own; it doesn't ask, doesn't reach; it moves like water, and just when you think you're on top of the wave, you're underneath it, turning over on your back, coughing and hungry for air. Outside time, outside the possibility of death when death is leaning in on you from the moon, the sky, the wires, the trees.

Then one night—why does it seem like it happens all at once when you know real change always takes its time?—you're no longer next to the conduit to your shared imagination, but lying alongside your damn sibling. You know him too well now to turn him into your projection screen, and what is a bigger killer of sex than familiarity? He is past and future. He is consequence, the other side of. And though familiarity might work for certain kinds of sex—say, intimate sex, after you've read a story to each other, or fought and made up, or shared something particularly intense, a secret—it doesn't always serve you when you're up for pure animal release, when you're an animal and you want another animal, without a context for you. The human version of the lyric bubble that Town can sometimes be.

Maybe all relationships, at whatever stage, come up against this koan, the riddle embedded in attachment—or is it just sex? And you find a way to stay fresh in the relationship, or is it the beginning of the way out, but you can't see it yet?

Candy

An easy morning, sun coming in through the frozen windowpanes. The two of us are still in bed. I'm reading a passage of a novel in which the word *intimacy* comes up. I read Noah the passage, a beautiful passage, not actually realizing that reading aloud to another is an act of intimacy until I'm well into the third paragraph. My voice isn't quite mine. My voice is just an instrument of the narrator's voice, the writer speaking that narrator, and I'm inside a box in a box in a box.

I lift my head to catch the look on his face, which I expect to be calm, in satisfaction.

"It's funny you have such a problem with intimacy."

I'm so confused by the outlandishness of the statement, the offhandedness with which it's uttered, I practically laugh aloud. Well, not aloud. It wouldn't be like me to do anything so mean. I turn my head aside, look down, as if to enact the designation. And that fills me with a rage that I can't help but turn inward, against myself. I don't want to be known to myself as someone filled with rage. Sorrowful—*hurt*—those would be better designations. But why am I participating in this pigeonholing? No one wants to be told he's one thing when he's already so many things, thick with contradictions.

"I don't understand," I say, my voice not terribly steady.

But he doesn't reply to that. He picks up a pillow from the floor and appears to move on to the tasks of the day. Rooms need to be cleaned, he has early check-ins coming before noon.

I try to mask the feeling from my face, but I know he must see it, feel it—I'm quieter than I would be otherwise. Is he asking for a fight? Have those very words been said to him before, in past relationships, and now he's turning them on me, to see what it feels like to wield them? It wouldn't feel like a big deal if it were said with kindness, with the possibility of hope and change. But there's accusation here, as if I were the one who were withholding sex. To me intimacy is sex, I can't disentangle one from the other. And if that's the case, I'd like intimacy all the time, first thing in the morning, just before brushing my teeth, and in the middle of the night.

I want to eat intimacy the way I want to eat candy!

It would be different if he'd said "we," right? A welcoming, an invitation. I can't see beyond my idea of aggression to grasp his statement as a key. I picture it on the floor of the bricked, circular cellar beneath this eighteenth-century house. It doesn't even occur to me to pick it up. I can't even see it as a way upstairs.

Talk to Me

There are examples of my type everywhere, in every city and college town, in every coffee shop and gym. He's always been around, across time. He has an extraordinary feature about him, a big beard, big ears. Whatever it is, he's an extraordinary animal. He stuns my attention, stills my wandering eye. I can't even read the novel in my hands without looking up every few minutes, if only to reassure myself he's as beautiful as I thought he was. It would be helpful if he had a nonexistent chin, or a stain on his shirt—everyone else in the room has no shine compared to him. I know he wasn't always this person. Possibly he was once pushed up against the lockers, knocked around. But the real point here? The guy won't look at me for even a second. All I really want is for him to see me, appraise me, dismiss me, look away—that would be just fine. But his demeanor, his attitude—he has no need of me. He's completely satisfied in his skin. He doesn't need to look outside himself for more. If I wanted to be cruel, I could think of him as incurious, a little dim, too controlled, self-disciplined: what horrible things are hiding in all that self-discipline? But that doesn't stop the animal in me from wanting more. From him? Ah, not even from him. This is just my fantasy of unworthiness, which I resurrect from time to time, to feel my limits, to feel alive. Sometimes it's important to sit with the thing that will never be given to us.

Subversive

The archetype is familiar: expressive younger man with a wild streak and a moneyed, alarmingly calm, slightly cold older man. I suspect Noah's ideal fits the designation of the latter, and Noah? Aside from the obvious stability, what could be in it for him? Maybe the wild one needs an opposite (an obstacle?) in order to cultivate his identity, his sense of self. Without the obstacle, how can he be subversive, maintain that role? What would he be? Would it feel like not getting a foothold in muck after the tide recedes?

It occurs to me one morning that I've been expected to play the stable part, even though I don't have money, even though I'm not alarmingly calm or cold, even though we're two years apart, even though I have plenty of a wild streak left, and want to protect it as much as he does his. How has this happened to us, to me? Maybe this is why Noah encourages me to keep a full beard when I complain it ages me. Or why he says he likes a small belly on a man when he's so devoted to keeping lean and fit, even shredded. In this equation the two of us can't be lean and fit, and what does that leave me? Here on out as a padded old man? Or the chance to rest, to live a little less, or a lot, because someone else is doing all the living for me. Someone else I'm expected to shake my head at in awe and affectionate exasperation to indicate I'm blessed. A little like the opening credit montage of *The Flying Nun*, in which the wise Sister Jacqueline shakes her head at Sister Bertrille and her high jinks—a comparison that would make Noah crack up if I ever mentioned it to him.

On some days I wonder whether a husband is always a variable integer for Noah. By that I mean his personality is far less significant than the role he's expected to perform. Maybe when Noah's walking down the street with me, he's actually walking with Henry, or anyone else who preceded me. Should that bother me? Maybe it doesn't as much as it should. I thought the point of growing up was to find your agency, to make choices and deal with the consequences of those choices, and the world I've put myself in is removed from all that. I've been captured by some category. Its arms are holding me too close. In lesser moments I think I might as well be that man with the jowls of a beagle crossing the street to get ice cream.

Speculative

Years from now I'll live in a place that thinks it's Provincetown when it isn't Provincetown. Yes, queer people and straight people will live side by side here, but there is no Provincetown when there isn't life in the yards and streets. In the pretend Provincetown, the citizens will stroll inside, pretend they hear a pot boiling over on the stove if they see someone walking down the sidewalk. They'll do anything, short of blinding themselves, rather than risk awkwardness, uncertainty. A spontaneous conversation? Backs will tense, not because these people are inherently cold, just that they know that human personality is disruptive and threatens the order they value more than they know. There will be a park, but it will be scraped clean with ballfields, more per square foot than any other place in the world—activity must replace spontaneity. There will be no halls of interaction, no bars, no coffeehouses, just churches. Instead there will be a farmers' market on Sunday to which people come after church to say hello and laugh, still under the spell of services or masses, and all their appeals to togetherness, which is where the divine lives. But the divine can be dangerous too— anyone who's held their hands over a fire knows that (the burn where your fingers meet your palms). Anyone who's felt it in the body of somebody else. The divine insists you stay awake because it can leave at any second.

I don't want to be superior to anyone for being afraid. We already have a culture built on that.

Boat

We're naked under the covers, the two of us, making the most we can of the lousy light. We're reading again: Noah from Elizabeth's first collection of stories, me from Joy Williams's *Breaking and Entering*. Our heads are filled with others' voices but we might as well be speaking those voices to each other. Noah latches his leg over mine and we drag closer. After a while Noah reaches up and tilts the lampshade to the right to see if he can get some better light. This could be enough. This could be the best any relationship gives any two people, and I don't know why I want to ruin it by asking for more. Will we always want more? His eyes look a little dazed, even dead. I can tell he's reading the same playful, nuanced sentence again and again, trying to get a hold on it and he can't, and soon enough he closes the book on the hardwood, turns on his side, and says, "Good night, honey." And I say, "Good night, honey." The room is absurdly still, not even a sound from outside, no wind or shutter banging or stones crunching under tires. I stare at the back of his head for a while. The clipped dark hair, so brown it's close to black, a gray hair here and there. A pink blemish, at the top of his neck, possibly a razor nick. It's a wonder I'm even here, sharing a warm bed with another human when I could be as alone as the hermit in *The Bride of Frankenstein* before he met his monster. The dead hover over and about us—maybe they are watching us through holes we can't see, maybe they're inside the light bulb, warming its thin glass. Can you hear them humming in unison? I hold that thought in my head for a while. I carry it along inside a little boat as I go under.

Prayer

Night up against the day, walk us into the next. Don't hold our stupidities against us. Forget them as you would the wind unless you think we need to be reminded of them. Don't let us forget the dead, and don't let us idealize them out of their humanness. Remind us of all the ways we're strong. Teach us to be useful, Night. Anoint our irreverence, our humor. Don't let us gloat when we're outspoken. Praise our anger and help us hold it inside our love. If this is the end, Night, calm and carry and lamp us forward. Fold each year of us into your nest so that time may not destroy us.

27

Parade

Noah holds out the chocolate cone to the girl, the vanilla cone to her brother. He seems perfectly at ease with serving soft ice cream to so many summer tourists, and he'd have to be to take this job. Binky's is right in the center of Town, across from John's Footlong, the Chamber of Commerce, a square freighted with park benches and gargantuan lobster traps in aesthetic formation. He works late hours, and after the place closes down for the night, he must stay another hour to swab out the machines. My ritual involves waiting for him, meeting him each night as he finishes up. We like these times. They give us simple peace at a time when simple peace is not to be found. Maybe this kind of thing is the best part of being with someone, but as the pleasure of it is modest, so self-effacing, we don't give it the credit it deserves, the way we do to a night of good sex or a happy vacation.

Carnival is the third week of August, and the centerpiece is a parade every year. It happens during the afternoon, though it used to happen at night, which Town stopped after the spell of darkness made things a bit raunchy and louche. Not to mention a particular incident in which activists in Town spontaneously kissed unsuspecting straight men on the mouth. It goes without saying that the men (and their wives and girlfriends) were convinced they'd been given HIV, even though everyone knew better by that point. I can almost picture them spitting the kisses out of their mouths, the screams and the cries. Human lives.

Did I mention the Buttlickers Unite signs? That too.

So it's all rather PG-13 these days, as family friendly as gay can be in the summer of 1993, during the hour of a plague. Noah will represent Binky's. He dressed up as Mrs. Binky the year before, which involved wearing a red-and-black checkered skirt, long black wig, black sunglasses, black high heels. Also a two-and-a-half-foot-tall vanilla ice cream cone balanced on his head. He will repeat the role this year, but he needs a Mr. Binky—will I do it? I've never refused an opportunity to be onstage, even if I am wary of the stage—at least before I go on. The plan is for the two of us to wear the cones on our heads. In addition to the cone, I'll wear a wig—a blond curly wig—and a white T-shirt, white painter's overalls, white Converse high-tops—I'm intended to be the man.

Which, let's face it, means boring.

Do I ever express the intuition that our costumes feel undercooked to me? What if we had a dog, a real baby, a hedgehog? I don't say so, nor do I bring any collaborating energy to the project. Maybe that's a sign of my unbelief, or maybe I sense that Noah doesn't want that kind of involvement from me.

On the afternoon of the parade, we mill about with the other participants outside Michael Shay's, the former Howard Johnson's. Noah makes a fuss over other participants, they make a fuss over him. Neither of us has bothered to practice walking with our ice cream cones, not even for a hundred feet, much less the length of the two-mile-long parade route. I haven't considered the rigors of balance, the possibility of a quick wind from the harbor, but summer leaves no time for questioning, pondering, worrying, speculating, rehearsing, getting it right. We're living right inside the moment. We are always running to work, whether it's waiting on people, folding sheets and towels, answering memos. There isn't a spare minute in the day, *literally*: Town leaves no room for practice. It's the Town of the first draft, and there's no time for taking out the gushy superlatives in paragraph two.

So many participants packed in the parking lot. Town's proportions radically redistributed—put twenty-five percent of the population in one place and it's different. It never occurred to me until now that my sense of Town has always depended on certain disbursements, crowds in the middle, or at Spiritus, and now that there are hundreds out here, it feels like everyone has gathered on one side of the raft and the raft is about to sink. There is excitement, buzz, a sense of competition keeping us all on our feet. Barbara Cohen takes our picture, and we don't yet know it will end up as a piece of art, later sold as a refrigerator magnet.

The parade starts. Noah walks ahead of me, strutting in those high heels, waving at people, in character, at ease with the hungry crowd. My cone topples off, falls to the pavement by my feet. I look up at Noah. I am mortified, and I don't have the stage presence to make a joke of my mishap, or go right on with the show. I am overwhelmed by all those eyes. I thought I was used to people looking at me, but it seems I'm not. If I were performing some other role, say reading from my work, or even teaching, I would know what to do. It feels like the toppling is connected to some secret instinct in myself that is driven to ruin, an instinct I've caught in others. Maybe I'd feel differently if I liked my costume, if it made me look remotely handsome in the way Noah's costume makes him look beautiful and sly, someone you'd want to get to know. I look like a lost and failed Bee Gee, a Gibb who wants to be onstage, but once he's up there, he sings a shade under pitch, embarrassing and infuriating his harmonizing brothers.

There's loud music behind us, a float—will big tires run us down if we stop? There are faces, seemingly thousands of them. It's best not to make eye contact with the faces, but it's hard not to. The faces aren't exactly supportive faces. And they're not homophobic, but they're starving for entertainment, stimulation, and spectacle, starving for us to do something *gay*, but not too gay, in order to take the gay out of themselves—if someone else could be a great big sissy for you, then why the hell not let him? They're not on our side, and until then my experience of straight suburban visitors to Provincetown has been: we might not exactly like you, but we are at least on your side. I look at one young man's face, and he looks back at me with the face of someone who wants to shoot a poison dart at my cone—the residue sliding down my forehead into my eye. And my relationship to my cone is tainted now: I've been thinking too much. I put it back on, try to walk with it for a few feet more, I bend my legs, tip my head just slightly to the left, and off it falls again.

"Fuck," I cry. "*Fuck!*" And again and again and again.

The cone is alive. The cone has a personality. The cone is not my friend. The cone wants to humiliate me. Once it knows it can fall off my head, it throws itself off as if to remind me it was never an extension of me, and I never had the right to assume mastery of its weight.

I hate my cone. I want to demolish it as it's demolishing me. It makes my neck ache. If it were possible I'd leave the parade route, find a baseball bat, and smash my cone to a thousand pieces until it was just useless pieces of plastic.

Halfway through the parade—I think we're there. Yes, Town Hall's just ahead, and Noah's disappointment is clear behind his wave and his wide, wide grin. I know his disappointment isn't simply in me; it reaches beyond me, and soaks into us. Maybe it's impossible not to feel disappointment after being taken in by all those eyes. All those eyes have taken some force out of us, and all that's left is a desire to forget. I wouldn't even call it emptiness.

I'll wake up tomorrow and I'll be the same, Town will be the same. But each time I drop the cone, I lose a bit more of the me I thought I'd built up in Town. I'm getting back the life I thought I'd left behind, the life of awkwardness, diffidence, errors. Sickness too.

And I'm no longer safe in my refuge. I've been taken out of my house and these visitors have brought their rules, their fear of shame back to me.

Why don't I take off the cone, hand it to someone, walk on, and at least have some fun with this time now that there are only a few blocks left? No one should take a parade, much less themselves, so seriously, but I'm too caught up in some act of loyalty to Town, loyalty to Noah.

I look up to see the people I know—Jim and Al, for instance, look at me with pitying smiles. The pain's about them, too, as no one's exactly having fun. The look in their eyes suggests we'll remember all this but we'd prefer to remember something else. Joy, for one, but joy doesn't etch its letters on your brain. Rather, the brain wants hurt, wants to hold on to it, as it contains the possibility of work, negotiating with it over time.

The cone falls six times. It's part of a routine now, as reflexive as a cough.

At parade's end, Noah doesn't talk. We are exhausted, dehydrated. There is no elation, no fun, no relief that's it's over, no adrenaline. We don't join any of the other revelers but merely walk away from the parade down Pleasant Street. We fold our arms close to our bodies, as if keeping ourselves protected and warm, though a cold breeze hasn't blown in hours. And Noah doesn't even have the energy to look at me.

"We got through it," I finally say, though I don't quite yet know why that feeling should be so important to see and say. We'll get through other things we can't even imagine yet.

28

Friend

Mark calls one morning, asking if I'll drive him to Hyannis. His car is at the Barnstable airport, and he's left it there out of some complicated travel scenario. On the drive down Route 6, I'm surprised by how comfortable we are with each other, how easily our conversation moves back and forth, without awkward pauses. We laugh a lot. We finish each other's sentences, as they say, which is a bit of a surprise, as I've always been in awe of Mark. Not just of his poems but of his command of the room at readings. "He's big," says David, another poet in Town. Another says, "He's blowing up," which seems remotely crass to me, as most of the poems are written out of the landscape of the Epidemic, navigating the inevitable loss of Wally. How do you love someone you're going to lose? his poems ask. How do you participate in life, all the way down to the work of perception, as in how you see this green crab's shell? "A Greco-Roman wreck, / patinated and oddly // muscular." His poems are meaningful not just to other partners of the sick but their parents and siblings too. There isn't very much out there to give people company, at least when it comes to words or songs or movies. News stories, accounts in magazines, but statistics? They don't see into your suffering.

Pitch pines flash by. The big sign at the Wellfleet Drive-in: my eyes drift to what's playing on the marquee. The two-lane Suicide Alley. Do we eat somewhere off the Hyannis Rotary? Possibly. Up until now I've really been only a friend of Wally's, and now it's a relief to know I have another friend too.

Somehow we never get sick of each other on that hour-long ride. We never run out of things to say, even though we don't say the first word about what's going on at home. We don't need to.

A few days later I get a phone call from Mark. Wally can't be left alone at home anymore. He's going to have full-time live-in help now, and they won't be needing me to check in on Tuesdays. He thanks me, and is too harried and distracted to say much more.

Hurt

I cannot know what brings it on, but one day the sentence comes out of my mouth, as if it can no longer be trapped. "Noah and I don't have sex. We stopped having sex months ago." The confession isn't exactly received as a shock by Polly. The calm, sympathetic interest on her face says she's heard such things before—or knows it herself? But to say it aloud burns the sound of the words into the atmosphere. To say it feels like no change is possible, and I'm helping to make sure we never have sex again. It comes with a little shame. I know it reveals that the two of us don't talk about deep things, how we might negotiate problems, grow with them. It's easier to rely on our routines to hold the two of us together. Plus, maybe I find it easier to grasp on to the fact that he doesn't find me attractive any longer and thus I can use that as an occasion to feel hurt, and then resentful. That feeling hurt: Hurt is my biggest drug, even though I don't often say that to myself. It's always so tempting to go there, to get that surge, that fix. What else out there, aside from sex, makes me feel more alive from the inside out? What else tests my resilience, reminds me of it?

It's preferable to simply decide we are happy, because in many ways we are—absolutely. And it feels important to demonstrate that we're happy when the culture tries everything it can to extinguish the queer couple. No legal protections. Just try to visit your partner when he's in the hospital.

A couple of days after my confession to Polly, it becomes clear that Noah has his own ideas about this situation, but he does it through humor, and channels it through somebody else. "Poor Paul," Lark will say to me in front of Noah. "Poor horny Paul," and I'll look down at the wood grain on the kitchen table and turn bright red. I'll laugh along, relieved to laugh the awkwardness away, relieved that Noah has seen the situation as important enough to discuss. Every time I've tried to bring it up, it's been waved away as if it's nonsense, a nuisance like a housefly darting about. I hear understanding in Lark's statement, but only some. He's making fun of me, but in a way that wants to include rather than exclude me. It says, Welcome to being a grown-up, welcome to getting less than you think you deserve. And you better start laughing now, turning the situation into a Borscht Belt joke, because you have no idea of the things to come.

But why shouldn't I think everything has been for sex? Isn't that what we've been dying for? Isn't sex more precious because we're always on the verge of being denied it? If there weren't AIDS in the picture, would these questions mean so much? Could AIDS make me want sex more than I would otherwise?

For its power, for its danger and rebellion.

India

Noah must be desperate to get away. Even though I love Town, it gets to be too much for me, and all I feel are its tight borders, that cold deep sea on three sides working on me like a ring I can't pull off my finger. He suggests spending the winter at my parents' house in Florida. I'm not sure he even likes what he hears about my parents; he thinks I'm not out and open enough to them. Sometimes I think the only parents he might like are so open-minded they don't exist in the world—at least they won't spring to life for another decade or so. And when they do, it will be as if supportive parents of LGBTQ children always existed but were too shy to let themselves be counted and known.

It's impossible to imagine Noah in my parents' Florida. When he hears "Florida," he likely sees palms and chickee huts and beaches—a failed take on Goa. I don't know how to communicate that my parents' house is another place, a new town spun up out of live oaks and sandhills a few years before: sprinkler systems, frenetically neat Floratam grass, white tile roofs, humans inside their houses or around their caged pools. The occasional armadillo or opossum. A pygmy rattlesnake. An hour from the nearest gay bar and gay neighborhood. A ten-mile drive to the beach, a listless Gulf beach, with sticky, greased barbecue grills and swings, mysterious shine fish slipping alongside your legs, a mile-walk out just to get deeper than your waist. I see him trying his best the first week, then getting bored, resentful, isolated. Who in this part of Florida would welcome him, would understand his humor and play? Perhaps my mother would. After a bit she'd come to care about him, want to be entertained by him, but she'd never be enough audience for him, and of course they'd get on each other's nerves, if not openly about it to each other, but to me.

What would we be without Town? We are parts of its body now. We are its lungs and feet, but our identification has come at a cost. We can't live anywhere where the climate conditions are less than hothouse ideal. We fear it's weakened us, taken away the armor we would have developed if we'd been living elsewhere. So where does that leave us? New York? Too expensive. Montreal? Freezing cold. Los Angeles? Amsterdam? San Miguel de Allende? Puerto Vallarta? Vieques? Tangier? Bali? Noah periodically brings up rural India, and I only wish he hadn't told me so much about his year of travels there. It all concentrates into a bus ride through the mountains, where Noah pushed himself down the aisle of the bus, crying for the driver to stop, and squatting in a gully to take a big watery crap as the people in their seats looked down and looked away in disgust. To Noah travel must feel like aliveness. In new circumstances, you're learning how to eat, how to accommodate the needs of your body. Maybe, on a deeper level, it involves saying fuck you to your old expectations, to realize that your manners were part of a system that told you that you were a loser, a good-for-nothing faggot, you were always less than useful, and thus you never got the opportunity to grow your strength.

Right now I don't have the energy to put myself through any of that. Palm trees, beaches, eighty-eight-degree water, mountains, yes. But hardship? I've lived too much of my life inside that word—or at least under the threat of it, which is its own kind of punishment. I don't want it to be too familiar: I want to shake it off. And aren't we living *hardship* in utopia, even when we tell ourselves it's home?

Speculative

What becomes clear is that I can't bring Town to another place. I can't grow a different body if the skeleton has already hardened.

What's missing in the Hypothetical Place? Sex. By sex I don't mean fucking. Sex will likely take place inside the houses, on the beds and staircases, but it isn't talked about. In Town sex is walked down the streets. I'm talking about the eros that keeps people alive, that connects us to others, to animals, to plant life. That takes us out of ourselves and does the same for others. An eros that's central to our lives as much as making things, paying bills, going out with our friends for dinner and drinks and movies. In the speculative place, bodies are shunted away. Death is directed to funeral parlors where bodies are perfumed, polished, powdered, fragranced, drained, pumiced—turned into something ghastly, as if the body were an aberration, as if death didn't happen to all of us, as if it were something to be embarrassed about. So much effort to sweep death to the sidelines when that place is all about death. It doesn't even know that death has always been our sibling.

Joy Williams: "death's energy, death's *vital* energy, is being ignored."

As to what is gained by this erasure? Privacy. All you have is the silence around your own body, your own head and hands. Ugly voices, rude people: If you put a headset on, you don't even have to take them in. Walk straight ahead, eyes straight ahead, cold. You know the type.

Which might be why I take the wrong turn when I'm visiting the Hypothetical Place on a trip. I don't drive down the outer lanes, where I'm supposed to go, but right down the center, which is divided by an abandoned railroad track. There's no way to get back to the outer lanes. There are curbs on either side, walls of tall shrubs, high as a one-story building. I've strayed outside my category. I drive faster and faster, there are ruts in the gravel now, I'm sure I'm going to break the axle in half. But a turnout appears and I wrench the wheel to the right. Disaster averted. I get out before the train heads south, but that doesn't mean I'm not shaken and humbled by my inability to see.

Unspoken

Lands End Inn perches at the top of the tallest dune in the West End, a bit country club, more Monterey Peninsula than New England, with an octagonal observation tower overlooking the hump of the mainland. The annual holiday party is tonight, and Polly, Noah, and

I climb the stairs from Commercial Street, drawn to lively voices, the music from the open windows up above. Every year David, the owner, throws open the doors of his guesthouse, and all the hardcore townies are there, from overlapping social circles. Tensions release as soon as we step inside. It's as if I don't know what I've been missing until I step inside. No one's drawing lines around themselves—or maybe they're just relaxing old lines. Everyone is safe—relatively. Unlikely conversations take place between unlikely people, and the spirit of that feels contagious. I wander away from Polly and Noah and end up talking to some guy I've seen at the gym for months but have never more than nodded to. It doesn't bother us that the food is freezer burned, or that the punch is suspect, as if some houseboy opened some cabinet and poured in all the liquor and mixers previous guests left behind. We think of its failures as endearing, even funny, even though David's health is reportedly taking a turn. We're riding the wave of death, and the party is meant both to distract us from that wave and to raise a glass to everyone who made it (or not) to another year. Everyone is recorded, remembered. And that is the unspoken story of the night.

Birthday

Maybe twenty of us crowd into Mark and Wally's tiny dining room, before the blinking, tinseled tree. It's coming on Christmas, but it's also coming on Wally's birthday, so two days are celebrated at once. A new dog has entered the household, a golden retriever puppy named Beau, who's so wound up—all these strange people in his strange new house—that the party ends up being entirely his: he's always knocking over a lamp or a candlestick, which provokes loud, joyous responses that try to mask alarm—doesn't Mark have enough to deal with without this wired and panicky animal? But there is genuine cheer in the room, even if the real guest of honor sits with an uncharacteristic quiet in the corner, paler than the Wally I know. Almost still. These are all people he loves to be around, and I'm not even sure he knows who we are. He tries for a smile every so often.

29

Merry Christmas

My parents' Florida isn't the Florida of Miami, Naples, or the Keys, whose climates take to aralia and Bismarck palm. I brazenly push the plant hardiness zone, buying plants that need to be tented, protected in burlap when the temperature falls into the high twenties. My plants have all the flamboyance of wet wigs. They are the plants of drag. They're leafy, spiky. They contrast greenly against the grass outside their lanai, which already looks arid, nipped by a flash freeze, even though the date is December 23. I know what I'm doing is bound to fail. It will take so much attention to maintain and preserve it, and is my mother up to the task of protection when I'm gone? We'll lose everything, but in the meantime, the yard is a dream space, rich with moisture, growing like crazy when the heat in that sun is on and on and on.

I stab the shovel into the impoverished soil, which has all the nutrients of a Provincetown sand dune. Beneath that, there is the thinnest tablet of limestone. My parents' house is in the sinkhole capital of Florida, but they don't know that yet. In a matter of time people will wake up to the sounds of groaning drywall and lumber, and if they're lucky they'll make it through the front door before the house is sucked into empty earth. Later, south of Tampa, a grown man won't make it alive out of his bedroom. That part of the house falls right into the earth, and his body is never found, despite massive and superhuman effort.

Can my mother see that I'm distracted, waiting for the minute when I can steal away to the unfurnished back bedroom and make that phone call? Her pressure fixes on me, even when her eyes are elsewhere. Occasionally she looks at me as if there's something wrong with me, as if I could be holding a secret inside. That look—it just makes me want to hide even more. I'm worried that if I do get an opportunity to make that call, Noah will be out, and I'll get the answering machine, leave a things-are-just-fine kind of report in a rapid, distracted voice that will inevitably sound like I'm missing him too much. It will sound as if we've been dating just six days rather than a full six months. In truth, my displacement has done something scathing and dangerous to time. It's tossed me back ten years—more. And it isn't just my parents' presence, no—it has something to do with the place: isolation, and the manufactured current of air-conditioning that is all about keeping us apart, making sure we're comfortable so we forget we have bodies that could get us in a bit of trouble. In terms of life experience I am seventeen all over again, with all the uncertainties of that age. I find myself snapping at the most minor thing (why *can't* I take the garbage out in five minutes?), and I can't stand the way my temper vanishes my dignity—and where is my sense of humor? It's awful to be reminded that what we've made of ourselves is so flimsy. Can be lost in all of two minutes.

Have I told Noah not to call me here? It's likely I've said such a thing, or more likely, implied it, and I can't imagine that making Noah so happy. Perhaps in his mind he's holding me at some distance for telling him I'll be hard to reach for the next ten days. Though I've lived in Town for two years now, deep in my muscles I still have the fear that my life is only a mirage. Maybe it's only something I dreamed up, an act of language. And maybe I can undo it all by leaving for ten days. What if everyone's dead upon my return? Toxoplasmosis, pneumocystis. The locks broken on my apartment, my books and clothes thrown out, nobody around to speak up for me or protect me or remember my name.

If a person is lucky, he outgrows those kinds of attachments, though that isn't the same thing as falling out of love.

I haven't outgrown my attachments, not at all, and when Noah answers the phone, it's clear his head is in a different place—he's experiencing none of my anxiety. He's not missing me. He sounds like he's having the greatest week in Town, where he's staying in my apartment with Robert, a friend of his from Toronto. Robert is a great guy, funny, tall, and magnetic, with a shock of fiery red hair. They've gone to some parties. They've had sex in my place— does Noah actually say that? It's quite possible I conjured this up out of paranoia, but if he did say it, he said it with the detached cheer of one who says he just loaded the gravy, the cranberries, and the stuffing into the Tupperware.

If my brain had a throat it would be caught in itself right now.

Outside the window the surface of the pool sparkles in its screened bronze cage.

Possibly Noah is waiting for me to react. And maybe he's angry that I'm not reacting, that I haven't stopped him from listing the mail that's come for me in our PO box. Maybe he finds me weak for not reacting. But I'd be an idiot not to cover myself with padding right now. And there's nothing I can change from here.

See? I shouldn't have come here. Merry Christmas. But if he thinks I'm a weak person? *Really?* My heart speeds up at the very thought. I am the strongest person on earth. Do you want to talk resilience? I'll show anybody resilience.

I picture telling him, upon my return, that I had sex in Tampa. I'll say, Beautiful, dark-haired guy, dark beard, muscular, the biggest, fattest cock in Tampa, always hard and ready to go again. But he'll see right through my story. He'll put an arm around me, pull me into his shoulder, as one would a teenager who dropped the football at the high school game, and feel sorry for me for being such a lousy liar.

Uncle John

Uncle John haunts and hovers over me like my mother's worst possibility for my future. She'll bring him up from time to time, and at other times I'll feel her keeping her hypothetical fear trapped inside, but why? She loves Uncle John and calls him up to check on him, calls whenever she's lonely and needs someone to talk to, but she is clearly repulsed by Uncle John. By his never being married, by his lack of a driver's license, by his attic one-bedroom apartment in Collingswood, by the electronic keyboard she bought for him (which he's never taken out of the box), by his elderly girlfriend, Marian, with her stiff frosted wig. By what he says to her about me when she's worried: that I'm weak and self-deceived. Uncle John = an inability to grow up. Uncle John = too passive to line up inside the expectations of adulthood. Uncle John = his fedora with the light halo of oil in the sweatband. Uncle John = unclean, no matter how many times he takes a bath.

She'll continue to be repulsed by Uncle John after his other niece, Jean, offers to put him up in her tiny ranch house in Pompano Beach Highlands. She won't hear the derision in her sympathy when she talks of his disastrous train trip down when he was too stricken to move from his seat, even to go to the bathroom, or when Jean forces him to give her power of attorney, or when she refuses to answer the door when my mother shows up unannounced and knocks and knocks and knocks.

Uncle John, who dies alone in Florida, without companions, but only a niece who turns instantly into a monster once she senses financial opportunity and a chance to strike revenge at her family, her history, and a lifetime of low wages.

Uncle John: is that only another name for my mother, and she needed to foist the drama of that on me?

No wonder I'm relieved to fall into community.

I am no Uncle John, which has been my life's work.

Hollywood

Noah and I sit in the left side of the Wellfleet Cinemas, not so far from the front. Though showtime is almost twenty minutes away, the theater is packed. I've never seen every seat filled, especially in the dead of winter on the Outer Cape. We're here to see *Philadelphia*, the first big-budget movie about AIDS. It has real stars, people whom everyday people like: Tom Hanks, Denzel Washington, Joanne Woodward, Antonio Banderas. Bruce Springsteen sings its theme song, "Streets of Philadelphia." I'm skeptical about it as I'm skeptical about all things Big—Big songs, Big novels, Big ideas, Big countries—all things Big have an inborn arrogance to them. As well intended as they might be, they are finally about wealth, accumulating it, and I can smell the machinery that wants to draw people in, that wants them to keep coming back. Big statements aren't for people like us; they're for people who see movies just to talk about movies—such as why you'd see a football game. They are for people all too happy to feel pity for people *over there*, miles away from the epicenter, *anyone not them*. Big statements hold a wet fingertip out to the wind. Big statements are inflected with a certain kind of self-congratulation, moral superiority. They'll say: We have cared for you all along, when you know the truth was always more complicated. And how could Hollywood not get it all wrong, turn the dying into saints, engraving in us the predictable cathartic responses?

On the other hand, it's a relief to be seen—queer people, people with AIDS, survivors, HIV-negative people: all of us. How long have we been erased? And if we haven't been erased we've been represented as depraved, weak. Not that some of those representations aren't hilarious: Joel Cairo in *The Maltese Falcon*, Sebastian in *Suddenly, Last Summer*. Enough.

The theater goes dark. I'm watching characters move across the street, but thinking more about Noah holding my hand, rotating the knuckle of my thumb with his own. Is there anything more satisfying than having your significant other holding your hand out in public, at a movie? Straight people take this for granted, but queer people? We can hardly wait for the lights to go down, and once the movie gets going, the real happiness begins: Noah's hand in mine.

But the film is so determined not to offend, not to get things wrong, it's managed to situate itself in a weird in-between place. It isn't exactly bad, but? I'm watching the way I would watch a documentary about dying dolphins. And I say that loving dolphins, but they're not me. Every time a potentially wrenching exchange happens on the screen, Noah squeezes my hand until it feels like the manual equivalent of Morse code. The movie isn't afraid to say, This Is the One Story of AIDS (no matter *Longtime Companion*, no matter *Brother to Brother*, no matter *The Man with Night Sweats*, no matter *The Body and Its Dangers*, no matter *People in Trouble*), and I'm annoyed that it doesn't intuit that there are countless stories that will never make it to the screen—stories of black, Asian, Latino people, stories of women. Hollywood has the power to sear a narrative into the collective imagination, and though I resent that power (what about all those film executives still in the closet?), I sit tight and obey. I won't start muttering complaints while I'm still in the theater.

And then? A man stands up halfway through the film—abruptly. It is a bright scene, as the whole theater is illuminated. He is crying like a baby, a baby boy, and it wouldn't be so wrenching if he weren't such a tough-looking guy, leather vest, Levi's, salt-and-pepper muttonchops. I've often seen him around Town, always in his leather bomber jacket and white T-shirt, always too butch to even look in my direction. He can't stand it—once you represent something it's real, and up until now AIDS has been only a horrible dream. Now he knows it's an emergency, and he stands up, weeping. I want to protect him. I want him to stop breaking my heart, I want him to keep crying, as nothing up on the screen feels as powerful as this, or the absolute discomfort of seeing it, listening to it. He walks out, breathless. I don't know whether he's crying for someone lost, or for himself, or both. Maybe he's crying because he thinks he'll have none of the people once closest to him (his parents, his sisters) when he dies, and he must suffer through this well-intended movie that insists every life is of purpose, every life shaped by logic. He has never known such good fortune. And if he should get sick? His friends? His friends, while well-meaning, might turn out to be flakes when they're most needed. They have bailed on him before and they'll bail on him again, and what should he expect when he's loved them for their spontaneity and quick passion and unreliability? Dependable people, as he knows, are boring people, and he knows what it's like to abandon others too.

For a while I don't see the man at the gym, at the A&P, or at the coffeehouse at the Mews. Not that I'm exactly keeping an eye out for him. That's just how it is when disappearance is as routine as breakfast.

Hayrides

Five thousand miles away, in West Hollywood, Louise Hay, a motivational speaker and writer, holds what she calls Hayrides in an auditorium. Every month nearly a thousand men with AIDS show up, some with their mothers, but never with their fathers, who wouldn't even think of coming. Louise Hay in a nutshell? You can heal your life if you change your thinking. Much of her vision revolves around statements like: My happy thoughts help create my happy body. Or: My self-esteem is high because I honor who I am. Some of the men hold on to the worn teddy bears of their childhood. The times are so grave and desperate, people are willing to find comfort and support anywhere. And they're not afraid to appear ridiculous, even if some accuse them of being in thrall to AIDS vampires, crisis junkies.

There is no Provincetown equivalent to the Hayrides—maybe there's just too much New England skepticism in the air, and besides, the AIDS Support Group sponsors dinners that people—positive or not—come to for camaraderie. But that's not to say that AIDS, the proximity to so much dying, can't make the best-intentioned therapist nuts. It gives some of them outsize presences, like cult figures. One draws closer than she should to her clients, visiting their houses, socializing with them, having dinner with their partners—what could professional boundaries mean in the free-for-all of this blasted world? She's never been closer to other human beings in her life. Her hair, her gauzy violet scarves—they all get bigger as she feels the old bonds blurring, her spirit swelling and opening up. The heat and intensity of being near the dying, the beautiful and young dying—the salve of bearing them through their passage. How could it not stir up the appetites?

The Giant's House
Disease has developed a taste for the bodies of the young and its hunger cannot be stopped.

Fee fi fo fum.

Death Notice
When I pick up the *Advocate*, the Town paper, I hesitate, then tear it open to the obituaries. Every news story, from the ads to the

articles about visiting artists, is subordinate to the obituaries—that's where the real interest in Town lies. I approach them with darkest anticipation, the way I might feel upon approaching the cooling towers of a nuclear power plant. On some level I must want to come across a name I know—as much as I don't, I really don't. It's like recognizing in myself the secret desire to find out I lost my wallet, so all my energy, my life force, can concentrate to a single point. And when I find a name, I read that person's story, the details of where he went to elementary school and college, what his favorite songs were—who were his dogs? There is the fresh pang of being alive in remembering that person. Oh—*that* guy! That guy with the orange streak in his hair, the blue bandanna carefully displayed in his right back pocket. He bagged my groceries at the A&P. Inevitably, there isn't a picture of him. All I have are the basics. It's like assembling a puzzle out of eyelashes and a scab and torn-off fingernails. When he looked at me last week I looked back at him, and we were both citizens of Town.

Scout

Not everyone who dies is a gay man. There is Scout, who washes the windows of several of the businesses in Town. She is booming and warm and in her body—dark blond and sexy in a soft, butch kind of way, with a magnetic mixture of feminine and masculine energy. She's probably about my age. She always looks at me like she enjoys seeing me, she approves of me in a way that goes beyond the mere biographical facts. Our social circles overlap. She's close to a number of artists and writers. And even though we have different expectations of our lives, we have plenty in common. She grew up outside Trenton, thirty miles north of where I grew up—and of course that's how I know that cadence, those wide-open vowels: "wooder" for water. One day she is parking her station wagon in Town, and then the next—pneumonia? No one ever uses the A-word in relationship to Scout but speculations are passed from person to person. Was she ever an IV drug user? Did she ever get seen by a primary care physician? If that beast could get Scout, sweet, sexy, strong.

Death after Death

. . . it starts to feel like life.

Or you've stopped being able to tell the difference. And in that way it doesn't feel like anyone ever goes away.

30

Cumberland Farms

Sometime after nine every night, Noah and I button up our coats and strike out for the Cumberland Farms on Shank Painter Road. We walk up Winthrop Street, by the cemetery, the oldest existing burial ground in Town, established in 1742. Its inhabitants aren't the newly dead but the old dead, who know there's been lots of activity in Town. Nevertheless they say: Don't forget us, those of us who lived long lives, long enough to lose our looks, our usefulness, our power. Not a car or another human in sight. Constellations appear: the Big Dipper, Orion. Darkness behind and ahead of us. Fox dashing into the brush. Once we're inside the store, which feels overlit after all that darkness, we go right to the Pepperidge Farm display and pick up a bag of cookies, cookies named Montauk, Chesapeake, Nantucket. They're likely spiked with preservatives, but it would be absurd to worry about preservatives at the end of the world. We're barely out of the store before we've torn into the bag, devouring them until there are just crumbs in the bag and in the whiskers around our mouths. We laugh about winter weight, but have six months to firm up before Noah is back on the go-go box. The night gets darker on our walk. We reach for each other's frozen hands and rub them warm. And this is why people couple up with each other.

Guesthouse

I have never met a dog who doesn't like me, but Zadie is no fan. She growls and threatens to bite me when I'm lying alongside Noah in his bed. And then she does bite me, not exactly breaking the skin, but scaring me, and the three of us are never exactly the same after that. I never know what part of me she's going to lunge for next: will it be a nip out of my arm, or my fingertip? My side? Throat? She just wants me to know she could hurt me if she wanted to.

Don't get too comfortable in my beautiful bed, sucker. I lie perfectly still, my heart beating, trying not to roll too close to Noah, to hold him or be held. I'm unsettled because I've always loved dogs, and she shakes up my sense of myself as a friend to the animals. And I feel like a trespasser.

Am I a trespasser? It *is* Zadie's house, Zadie being the innkeeper's dog, who's now attached herself to Noah, and vice versa. Once Noah took the job at this new guesthouse he stopped sleeping over at my place. In logical terms, he has a room of his own now, with a dresser and queen-size mattress on the floor. His move makes sense: that twin bed with the soft mattress was giving us both bad backs, and I was tired of slipping down into the space between the window and mattress. So it was decided I would go over and sleep at the guesthouse: a restored Cape Cod with wood beams, wide-plank floors, a fireplace, and glass bowls full of pears, oranges, and apples. The inn markets itself to a high-end crowd, hundreds more per night than the desperately randy Manchester Inn, which is as close as you could get to a bathhouse in Town. Here sexuality lives behind closed doors—no one needs to spell that out: the price and atmosphere assume you're in on the news. I would be foolish to balk about staying with Noah here. I'm getting two worlds, my privacy during the day, and nights in a snug, welcoming house, where visitors, excited about their stay in Town, sleep in the rooms to the right and left of us. Occasionally I run into some guest in the hallway outside, and we laugh sheepishly about seeing each other in our underpants.

I leave the guesthouse early, as I do every morning. The street is empty at 6 a.m., a few carpenters driving to the Lobster Pot for coffee and blueberry muffins. The sunlight holds cold in it. It seeps up my wrists, inside my coat sleeves, which trap it for a while. I'm used to feeling underdressed in New England, bearing into the chill, as if that chill is a test. I haven't even bought gloves this winter, and I think I might get through February without needing them. Already there's a richness to the light, a deep yellow warmth that rubs some of the hardness out of the cold. It gives you a positive and negative charge at once. Polarity.

A friend of mine appears in her truck just outside my house and parks. She sticks her head out the window to say hi and I might as well be naked. I haven't had coffee, haven't brushed my teeth or taken a shower—I would never take a shower at the guesthouse; I always wait until I get back to my own place. As a rule, I always leave the guesthouse before anyone I know in Town is up and about. I realize it sounds like sneaking around. Maybe that's a way to keep things fresh for myself so that our relationship doesn't feel so domestic, but tinged with the heat of an affair.

"He should come and stay with you sometimes," my friend says. She doesn't say it with judgment, doesn't suggest I am complicit, or that I am allowing myself to be pushed around—any of the things she could be saying. She says it with a big smile, lightness and play lifting her voice. It's as if she's already seen Zadie leave a red bite mark on my stomach. The tone is simply: *consider this.* And she won't judge me if she sees me coming home in the same spot, on the same street, a week from now. She's aware she has the power in this exchange, and doesn't want to impose herself.

That's it—it isn't about her but about me. And I love her for speaking up, as much as I could love someone I've never spent more than five minutes with at a time. She speaks up. She speaks up.

"You're right," I say. "Thank you."

The truth is, Noah hasn't stayed at my place in so long that it feels some allegiance has shifted. He isn't interested in the innkeeper, a fellow I've known in Town, in a sexual or romantic way. But Simon seems to have a hold on him that makes him feel like more than just another boss. Perhaps Simon is able to give something to Noah that I can't give him: a sense of rules, boundaries, expectations? And there I am with all my needs, though I put so much effort into suppressing and denying my needs. With Simon, at least Noah has a real home, but it's a home with freedom, without the usual encumbrances and obligations, which can take the joy out of being with someone.

It will take me years to find out that might not be a bad place to be. When I first came to Town I thought I needed someone else to complete me: I wanted a collaborator. I was hungry for some information and experience I couldn't possibly have grown up with, some negotiation and pushback. At a certain point I didn't need that anymore.

It's not that I was complete: who would ever be full enough? It's just that when I look at myself now I might be enough to myself.

Futurity

At another time, decades ahead, I'll be in the lucky position to think about the future. I'll be having that necessary conversation with my department chairman about reappointment and tenure, the procedures I need to go through to make that happen. In the days leading up to that meeting, I won't sleep through the night. I'll take an over-the-counter sleeping pill. I'll pee three times during the night at two-hour intervals. On the way to the meeting I'll notice my hands shaking. They'll feel ten degrees colder than my shoulders, which are furnacing. I'll sweat through the fabric of my shirt, and by the time I sit down with my department chairman I'll worry that the bacteria will betray me and I'll smell. I'll think of myself as a fraud. I'll think I have no right to be thinking of a future. Doesn't he know I've been dying all my life, since my twenties, and there's no way I can start undying now—even if I haven't seroconverted? It's too late to undo all that, don't put me through this, please. It hurts to be told I have more life to be accountable to, more calendars to manage. The person I have to be right now: he's only a phantom, an act of language; he's pretty good at appearing as someone with actual flesh on his bones, an expression on his face. And if he has to betray his relationship to time (leap of arrogance), does that mean the day ahead of him will be less precious, less singular? Will it lose its vibrancy and color? And, by turning toward the future, am I losing what's left of my youth?

To think I have all the hours in the world now. To think I was protected by time.

Ambition

I'm sometimes glad to think that in ten years I'll be dead. By then the only gay people left will be those whose lives were ruined by watching the rest of us die.

WALT ODETS, *In the Shadow of the Epidemic: Being HIV-Negative in the Age of AIDS*, quoting a twenty-three-year-old two weeks after an HIV blood test

The phrase can come up anytime, in the restaurant or at the beach with friends. Usually it's just when the two of us are together. "I have no ambition," Noah says. He says it as if his entire vision is represented by those four words. He says them with a tired smile. I don't think he wants to wield them as one would a weapon, I don't believe he wants me to hear them as aggressive, but he certainly must see the confusion on my face, in response. It feels personal, mysteriously—maybe I'm thinking only selfishly, and if I could only see around my feelings, I'd be detached enough to see that his feelings might have nothing to do with me. Why should I expect my presence to lighten his dark days? It doesn't occur to me to ask what ambition means to him. For me it is wound up in the stuff of purpose, agency—it's hard-won, and not necessarily corrupt. If his answer were, say, money and power and competition, the characteristics he associates with being a lawyer—I'd understand. I refuse that kind of ambition, too, but I think he's talking about a graver matter: the future, a sense of it being hopeless, a maw, an empty drain with no bottom.

One day I have a good writing day, and the increasing rarity of that kind of day is cause to communicate it. Noah's listening, his face intent, locked on me, though he might be asking himself, Why is he so excited? I'm glad he's happy, but does he have any clue that this makes me feel lonely, separate from him? I tell Noah that when it's going well I feel a little like God, and instantly Noah cries, "Paul," with such shock—his voice shoots up an octave, as if he'd watched me knock over an old man without apology. And shame cracks me apart, because I hadn't been prepared for any response but enthusiasm. What did I do? Maybe I sounded arrogant, blasphemous to someone who doesn't even believe in that kind of God, which is the worst kind of blasphemy. I should have said, I felt a part of God, or with God, or in God, but there's no way to take it back now, and the memory of the good writing day has evaporated. It's transformed into something self-involved and a little sinister, and I do whatever I can to speak in a more casual voice in order to pull the day back into a position where everything is just so. We eat and chat about who's checking into their rooms tonight. I'm still shaken. And God goes.

I'd understand Noah better if he were reading Thich Nhat Hanh: "Freedom here is freedom from craving, from anger, from hate, from despair . . . [pause] . . . from ambition. All these afflictions make you not free. The happiness of a person very much relies on her freedom. If you have . . . worries, anxieties in your heart, you are not free."

But neither of us is sitting with our Buddhist monks. We probably should be, but it doesn't occur to us to do that in a place in which we're supposed to be happy.

Would Noah have ambition if there were no AIDS in the atmosphere?

Axiom

Didn't Noah once say, "A couple has to want the same things"? We use that axiom to talk about the couples we know, especially the couples we've watched breaking apart, after a long time. Of course we're too much inside our own relationship to talk about us with any clarity, so we focus outward. "A couple has to want the same things." Whenever he says it, it hangs in the air for a minute, like a banner spun silently from a toy gun. X wants to be a writer, Y has no ambition. I don't want to make a math out of dividing these statements against each other, but why does Noah bother to stick around?

Runner

The trick is to disappear myself. At least this is what I think, as I walk back and forth in front of the crowd, holding a painting on either side. I'm working as a runner for the AIDS Support Group Auction, and my gut feeling is that a painting will have more power—and thus rack up bigger bids—if I try not to exude too much personality, thus directing more energy to the painting than to the look on my face. I hold the painting out in front of me, covering myself, which seems appropriate given the imperative of the cause, though we also want to make sure we're having fun. This one is a Duane Slick, a field of off-white on white, spread onto the canvas with a knife. We are halfway through the night, two more hours to go. How small can I make myself? Queer people have learned how to do that from way back. And the bids keep going higher and higher.

Harness

If he could look me full in the face and say, I want what you want, and say it with belief—would I be able to stand there and take it, all the way down into my heart? Would it disperse all my anxieties? Would it feel like I was finally coming home to my body, the fears of so many years arrowing toward that moment? Would I say, outright, You're here, and would it feel like more life, better life?

When Noah tells me I think of him as the "love of his life," he says it as if he's been sentenced, with only a bit of wryness mixed in. I can almost picture the harness around him—not the sexy kind of harness, but something an animal might be forced to wear until he stops kicking, relaxes into his punishment, and goes numb.

The love of your life = expectations. The love of your life = future together.

I have yet to rest in the harness of that statement, which I can't even say is true today. Maybe I'd feel it lifting me off the ground if the feelings between us were reversed.

31

Shaved Head

We're in a store, Polly and I, and just as we're heading for the door, I spot the back of a head on the closed-circuit screen. The hair is thinning on that spot and—*freeze*. It takes seconds to realize it's me. It hits me so hard that I almost gulp for air. My heart is broken. How could that balding man be me when my father, mother, two brothers, and uncles on both sides have the thickest hair, low hairlines? Is this what stress means? I didn't grow up to lose my hair, as do other men, who get accustomed to the idea through seeing who they might become through the examples of their relatives. My favorite men shave their heads, but it's different to imagine taking on that look for myself. After I get used to the inevitable, I'll have my hair stripped and bleached one last time until it's silver-white. Perhaps, without knowing it, I'm getting used to the idea of looking old while I'm still young. I enjoy becoming another human for two months (except for the special purple shampoo that can be bought only at a beauty supply store in Orleans) and then get sick of people talking only of my white hair and thick, dark brows. I have it cut off, without ceremony—and from here on out I look like Hollis.

Employee of the Month

When it comes to buying clothes, people are as unpredictable as the Outer Cape weather. Either they take up too much time or they don't take up enough, and I simply have to second their intuitions. If they're feeling enthusiasm, then I tell them they look great. If there's a dubious expression on their face, I shake my head, take the shirt out of their hands, and tell them I'll put it back on the hanger for them. It's surprising how quickly I take to selling clothes—and I'm grateful I get to work for Polly and my friend Stephen, who manage the place. There's no wealth of jobs in Town, and you're lucky if you're working in a situation that isn't downright abusive.

A year's worth of money to make in three months—the high rents. No wonder store owners are maniacs! For the people who walk through the front door, we do what we can to make the store look like fun rather than a duty, which involves wearing name tags with invented names ("Me Llamo Go Go"), pasting faces clipped out of newspapers onto dollar bills and handing them out as change, and playing music that might have a harder edge than what customers usually hear in other stores—say one of Millie Jackson's extended monologues between vocal tracks.

At the register, people don't really know if we're being serious or not in our conversations, and it makes them nervous.

Sometimes I just tell someone, "You don't really want that." I'd like to keep my job and collect unemployment for the dark months of winter after the store closes for the season, but it's for the sense of camaraderie. It's good to shake up the structure every so often, especially when the owners keep talking about implementing what they call the Up System, which essentially pits store clerk against store clerk, attaching a name to each sale, but without giving us commissions.

Unfortunately, the possibilities of transformation are too much for some people. For some, buying a new shirt is simply a matter of play, and for others? Those others can be so mean, with a coldness that resents me for being the one to remind them they have a body, and they'll never be their imaginary perfected self. Here, even the most confident person comes up against the fact that the inner and outer don't match, and if they have to blame someone, they'll blame me, as I'm standing right in front of them, and it's easier to believe the store is mine. They wouldn't even need clothes, dammit, if I weren't standing there trying to fan the need.

The people I like the best are these people, the ones I've had some tension with. People I haven't expected to like. This particular customer is someone I've seen in Town. She works at a gift shop not too far from the Work Center. I'm wary of her because she gives off the feeling of someone who's pompous, who takes herself way too seriously. Though she might technically live in Provincetown, she situates herself in another town, doesn't interact with my town, and would probably prefer that my town didn't exist. She picks up an overdyed violet sweatshirt. She studies it a long time—Town's name appears on the front—as if she needs to be reminded of where she lives and works. When she walks out of the dressing room, her head is down, there is such shame on her face. She says something about hating the size of her breasts. I don't know what to say to that, though the intimacy of it makes my face fall. There is heaviness and sorrow in her voice and it hurts. But within seconds she lifts her face to the mirror, and I can tell she likes the way she looks. All I say is "You look great." And I'm not merely telling her what she wants to hear. It's all true, the light in her face. Her intuition locks in at this moment and I'm its strike plate. Neither of us moves or talks for a minute. She stands before the mirror and says, "Yes, I do"—still testing out the idea, but on the way to being OK with it. And when she thanks me, she isn't being simply automatic, perfunctory. She means it. It feels good to be together, just for this moment. And every time I see her wear that sweatshirt down the street I'm back to when we turned toward each other, saw each other, and categories fell away.

Votive

On a cold night in January, Noah and I walk to a reading at the Work Center. A votive candle burns in Mark and Wally's window. Are we too scared to say what we think? Noah grips my bare hand harder, and just as we turn into the Work Center parking lot, Mike Mazur asks if I saw the candle in the window. "Have you heard anything?" he asks nervously, as if he's afraid to make something true by giving speech to it. "No," I say. And I'm moved he'd think I'd know, and I feel empty that I don't. A lifetime of changes can happen in a day. The reader's sentences are laced with rich descriptions and a careful attention to sonics, but I can't get the candle out of my mind.

Awkwardness, Please

The guy on the bed takes two breaths and arches his back almost imperceptibly, his lips slightly parted. I have hold of one leg and his sister one hand philip another hand or part of his arm and we're sobbing and I'm totally amazed at how quietly he dies how beautiful everything is with us holding him down on the bed on the floor fourteen stories above the earth and the light and wind scattering outside the windows and his folks at this moment standing somewhere on the observation deck of the empire state building hundreds of stories up in the clouds and light and how perfect that is to me how the whole world is still turning and somewhere it's raining and somewhere it's snowing and somewhere forest fires rage and somewhere else something moves beneath dark waters and somewhere blood appears in the hallways of the home of some old couple who aren't bleeding and somewhere someone else spontaneously self-combusts and somehow all the mysteries of this world as I know it offer me comfort and I don't know beans about heaven and hell and somehow all that stuff is no longer an issue.

DAVID WOJNAROWICZ, *Close to the Knives: A Memoir of Disintegration*

Fifteen minutes into the reading, I know life isn't happening in this space. I feel the walls of the Common Room closing in. The room heats up and one person shifts and others follow. Someone in the back row coughs and then another. Throats are cleared. A barely perceptible moan. If the reading were more awkward, if one section were a little slapdash, it might feel like life with all its co-incidences and accidents. I lean into Noah and he pulls away: the room is hot. Someone rushes toward the restroom, a toilet flush-ing, the door opens, the fan still roars, how annoying—ah, there it is, life. We have no time for empty ritual, all of us sitting side by side in this room.

Such are the demands of performance in a dark, dark age.

Some Change Went through Them All

Everyone in Town is here at the UU Meeting House—at least Town as we know it, people with associations to the art and writ-ing worlds. Chatter in the air, people walking up to other people, greeting and smiling, but with a sense of great sadness held back. It feels more like Christmas than a funeral, maybe because so many are used to going to funerals by now that they've been rewired—they look like something else. At times they probably catch themselves thinking they are at a graduation, a wedding, or an award ceremony until they realize that someone they knew, and maybe loved, is dead: chips and ash inside that porcelain urn up front.

Wally is in that urn, or pieces of him. I can't quite get my head around any of this.

I don't want to sit in this pew or have anything to do with it. I have been to other funerals, I used to be a song leader at funerals when I was young, but this is different. I know I'm holding Noah's hand, and I know people I know are speaking, people I don't know are breaking into song, and it all feels so loving, but I can't keep still in my seat. I smooth my brows. I'm usually the adult who gets annoyed when other adults are too distracted to stay calm and focused on the thing at hand, and here I am, behaving like someone I'd make fun of. My eyes wander over the tall white walls, the trompe l'oeil ceiling, the wall frescoes done in egg tempera. The building itself was built in 1847, but it's probably seen more funerals in the past five years than it saw in the twenty-five years before that. What does a building do with all that ceremony, that intensity? Does it lose its carbon, oxygen, and hydrogen? Is it still living, is it watching us? Do all the layers of feeling—or holding back that feeling—alter the composition of the beams, the supports, the floorboards? Do they soak up that residue and hold it, keep it inside like cold Atlantic water, or do they sturdy and flex, like a bulkhead against rising tides?

I could keep piling up metaphors when I know I should be present, know I should be thinking about Wally. Wally with his head on the pillow, Wally walking down Pearl Street with Arden. Wally in the garden. Wally making a joke about high colonics and cleanses. I can't.

Noah and I stand up. The service is over, people are walking out into the January cold, hugging one another, promising to stay in touch when they know they'll forget—and could you blame them, finally? I want to rush out the door, undetected: I have done my duty. But I know I must say a few words to Mark before we leave, even though I'm afraid, childishly afraid, in no position to put on the mourning suit of correct language. Even the pressed shirt, pressed pants, and tie I'm wearing feel like a fraud on me. How do others summon up the exactitude to say the right thing, when language, the one we've been given, offers us but ten words to make that happen?

Virginia Woolf, *To the Lighthouse*: "Some change at once went through them all, as if this had really happened, and they were all conscious of making a party together . . . on an island; had their common cause against that fluidity out there."

Noah is by my side. Polly there too.

I hug Mark. He feels taller than I remember him feeling—am I crouching to make him feel that way? I don't want him to feel any less than he is. And there it is: the stunning proximity of aloneness. When my senses are at attention it's impossible not to fall off the edge.

And suddenly I burst into tears, as Mark's body feels real to me, and I feel his body's ache, the body that knew Wally's body, and my tears aren't even about me, but what's to come: Lucy dying, Billy dying, Philippe dying, when do I stop? My mother dying. My father. Denise, my friend.

Getting together with Mark. Breaking up with Mark, eighteen years later.

The time line breaks, scrambles.

We're held up in the menacing net, over the void—I don't know what other name to call this space. Lives passing through that net— human, animal, plant, and molecules too small to see, which is another way to say *time starts here*. The clock is closer to an ending. We haven't been living our lives, though we certainly thought we were. And all this happens within sight of Noah and Polly, who look stricken, as if they see into something I can't yet see, or don't want to. The expressions on their faces pull me back to here. I wipe my eyes and nose on the back of my fist.

"Hold them while you can," Mark says, holding me a second longer, before letting me go, as if to point out what we already know—it's all provisional, it's always been in process. Even when people live and work together, share the same bathroom, same towels, same spoons and forks, same bed, and keep on living in tandem. There isn't a charm to ward any of it off.

Even if AIDS weren't in the picture.

There has been too much composure till now. I need to remind myself that I breathe, I have lungs I need to use again. I shift back and forth in my hard, stiff shoes, the shoes that somehow make my head ache. We smile good-bye and talk about staying in better touch.

Then I grab Noah's hand, swing it back and forth, and we're out in the day, cold, bright, astringent. And where do we begin as we walk past store after papered-over store?

32

In Between

And you pursue me. And I evaded you, as long as I could.

HUUB OOSTERHUIS, "And You Pursue Me"

There is a test, of course. The prospect of the test scares me because if I shouldn't get the news I want, I've lost my freedom. I still want to believe I can move into my life. And I still want to believe there's one more life after that.

But freedom? Maybe it's worse to keep worrying about the wave that will inevitably pull me under. It might be better just to get the news now. And maybe that's why some decide to forgo precautions. It's cruel to have only two countries, positive and negative, in which to live your life. I think of Thomas Mann's Doctor Faustus, who voluntarily contracts syphilis in order to get twenty years of inspiration.

If inspiration is a country, that's where I want to live out my days. Faustus: "Disease, and most specially opprobrious, suppressed, secret disease, creates a certain critical opposition to the world, to mediocre life, disposes a man to be obstinate and ironical toward civil order, so that he seeks refuge in free thought, in books, in study."

The truth of it has to do with my resistance to groupness. Maybe I just think I'm too good to be one of the herd. I don't want to join their weekly caravans to Boston, I don't want their generous therapists, I don't want their weekly dinners made with such love by the people in Town. I don't want their Christmas and Hanukkah parties. I don't want to be damaged and ugly. I don't want to be pegged down to this America, to this Mickey Mouse town, especially when so few countries will even let me across their borders. And just try getting back in.

No wellness without illness, I realize this now. The world was never merely divided into two columns. My body has always known this, but my brain was slow to catch on.

I'll go to the doctor only if symptoms present themselves. I will live in this in-between state for years and years, longer than I care to name. Maybe I will still be living like this when there's a cure—what, twenty years from now? thirty? At that point the skin of my neck might be so loose no one will want me anyway.

I must be attuned to my body, and that means everything: how I feel in my shoes, the color of my pee, the texture inside my mouth, my tongue. The taste of my breath—is it stinking? Does it taste of copper, of the pennies I stuffed into my mouth as a child?

It doesn't occur to me that I could be so strong I might not feel something wrong, even when it's there, *burning inside me, intimate as a lover.*

I'm a coward, a piece of shit. And I have as much integrity as any human could ever have under these conditions—I shouldn't punish myself. Some say I could pass on the virus to someone else, but I don't have sex that way. Well, most of the time.

I could live better, eat better food, exercise, hydrate, take better vitamins, do yoga, all of it. But is there a cost to giving up the body's pull toward darkness? The language of my dreams isn't always nice and kind. The language of my dreams is meat and sweat, hair and spit, bone hitting bone, ruthless. Can a body live without darkness? It might need darkness—or its brother, disorientation—just as it needs the light. The little punishments that give it so much joy, that test it, that make it hurt, dizzy—to let me know it exists.

Dana Spiotta, *Stone Arabia*: "I read somewhere that the brain needs disorientation to properly develop. That childhood desire to feel dizzy has something to do with increasing the vestibular and cerebellar interaction in the young brain. Proprioception is the activity where the brain orients the inside world with the outside world. Spinning throws off your proprioception and the brain works and develops as it tries to get it back. The desire to spin around is healthy, I guess, because it teaches the brain how to get a stable fix on the world under any circumstances."

As to the few friends who've taken the test: do they have a stronger need to be grounded than I do? Are they wary of spinning off and away, losing their coordinates, their grid? Of the ones who have tested positive, will their health insurance deny them coverage if they're lucky enough to have it? Will the drugs fail, corroding their kidneys and livers? Do they ever think they might be scooped up and put in a camp one night? Who knows with this government? Once one evil disappears, another evil takes its place, and what better vulnerability to fix on than AIDS with its metaphors of invasion, so close to paranoia, the fear of the immigrant, the foreigner?

Is it exhausting to live like this? How does it wear me down, bleach my thoughts away like sun on a patch of rug until I am no color? Does it leave me stupid, without much room left for an animating thought?

Swallowing, I feel a sore throat coming on one morning. I drink tea with honey. I take another spoonful of honey; I decide I'm dehydrated. But the sore throat won't go away. I've tried to take the vitamins, tried to gargle with saltwater. Chloraseptic. The Sucrets of my childhood. Megadoses of fizzy vitamin C water. Granted, I've been staying out too late and have been on my feet all day. It will kill it out of my system. When I go to Outer Cape, it doesn't help that I'm asked questions with a gravity and concern that suggest my illness could be attributable to only *one thing*. When I say no to the doctor's long list of questions, he doesn't offer to give me an HIV test. I would've taken the HIV test. Maybe he's not allowed, maybe that wouldn't be done during a routine visit. But the visit has a stink to it. A foul-smelling cloud follows me out of the office and that cloud seems to stay with me for hours into the next day. It smells like a sock, a worn sock that no detergent can get the smell out of, even after it's been washed a dozen times.

That night, sitting on the post office steps, I'm miraculously better, so much better. (You think I have AIDS? What AIDS? I'll show everybody I don't have AIDS. I have never felt better in my whole fucking life.) I tell the story of the doctor's visit to my friend, but others are in earshot. One person doesn't look at us, she looks straight ahead, but smiles, to indicate she is an ally. The manner of my report is suddenly shot through with indignation, outrage. Can't a queer man even stub his toe without some well-meaning idiot attributing it to HIV? What if I went into the waiting room with a bee sting, a hangnail? *Jesus.* We laugh some, flabbergasted but not exactly shocked. But my indignation feels larger than just me. It crests on a high wave of its own. Anger is so complicated that it belongs in many places, fills many rooms and houses, all over Town and beyond.

Sharrow Vale

An entire novel comes to me one day, at least in my imagination, and in this scene a man sits on the sofa. He has been sitting on that sofa so long he's not even sure his legs are going to move when he finally gets up. It would be so easy to get up, so easy to wash the dishes in the sink, pull some weeds from the joints between the bricks in the patio, dust the stairs, but to do that he'd be giving in to superstition. His boyfriend told him he'd be back from the doctor hours ago, and it is dark. It has been dark for two hours, fifteen minutes. Why didn't he go with him? He puts his hand in the fur of his dog. Has his boyfriend been in an accident? Too many people getting into accidents on Route 6, people driving with such recklessness as if that patch isn't ghosted or cursed, so they're still racing right through it. He can't stand this waiting, especially in the wake of this rough week, when his boyfriend's reported he's gone to get an HIV test, done this without consulting with him first. Shouldn't they have been tested together? Since then he couldn't do his taxes, couldn't finish a single article in the newspaper. Distraction has been his job all week, and it's both saved him and done him in. There's nothing worse than jumping up every five minutes, and he's not jumping up now. Headlights drag a reflected square near the ceiling, from one side of the room to the other, over the hutch. The engine doesn't make the sound of his boyfriend's engine. The dog knows: he hasn't jumped up in awareness, anticipation.

"When we find out I'm negative we won't have to use those anymore," his boyfriend had said, pointing to the unopened condoms on the nightstand. But the man couldn't summon up enthusiasm then, and can't summon up enthusiasm now. The space between the test and the results is a deep and sharrow vale. And dread shatters sex, any images related to it. It turns the body into a brain. The brain swells and shrinks private parts, along with animal needs.

A car door slams, the dog barks and lunges at the window. Panting in the room. Oily, hormonal smell. Rather than follow the dog to greet his boyfriend, he will sit where he is beside the lamp. Bad luck to walk to the door with the expectation of good news on his face. Bad luck to look like worry is etched around his mouth. He will stay where he is, holding the pillow over his stomach, and wait for his lover to open the back door and walk into the living room.

His boyfriend's face is not smiling. He nods up and down, and it is not the face of the man he was but the face of a boy, the face of someone who is scared, so scared. The boyfriend sits down beside him. The man collapses over him, into the heat of his lap, and wails. It is not the wailing of someone from the movies, say, a character in *Philadelphia*, but someone who's completely in his body, and sees himself alone, just the way his boyfriend was alone, when he lost his late lover. If he'd already prepared himself for the worst news, would he have been in better possession of himself? The world is not supposed to be as dark as they say it is. All his worrying about the dark was really preparation for the light, right? Somehow he thought they'd escape it. What arrogance to think they'd escape it when New York City is dying, when Africa is dying, San Francisco, West Hollywood, Amsterdam, Haiti, Moscow, Dublin, even the guy across the street visited by the flashing but silent ambulance the other night. When the man raises his head from his boyfriend's lap, each object in the room burns with such magnificent force he's surprised they haven't exploded in tandem. All the while the dog of black curls stands before them, head down, head pressed into the couch, wagging his tail as if that moving from right to left, right to left could possibly make things better in the room.

33

Null

"This," Noah says. "What is this?"

Lack of specificity pulls everything into it, like a drain. It sucks down all of the characteristics out of his room. And all we have left is our bodies, taut and alert.

The look on his face, this voice—they're not his, they don't belong to a person who insists on lightness, a person critical of anybody taking himself too seriously. The voice has gravel in it, age. Rage, too, as if cleaning rooms and attending to guests' needs should be enough. Why should one extra thing be demanded of him?

The look on his face—I don't know what to do with its inwardness, inscrutability.

"This—" he says again, tossing his hand up. "Us. There's nothing here."

A curious calm, as if we've slipped into a movie of animals. In thanatosis animals fake death in order to get a predator to leave them alone. Is he a predator now?

Then I get it. Us. The two of us.

He doesn't say he's unhappy, doesn't say there's a hidden boyfriend, doesn't say he's moving back to Montreal to go back to Henry or even to his family.

Then emotion feels stacked in a way that there isn't a single word for, because it has too many layers. Unhappiness? It would be one thing to hear he was unhappy; I could take that. Unhappiness could be examined, cut up on a table for study as in a biology class, but—he's never let on till now.

We try to talk it through, but it's all hunches, stammering, simmering, red faces, urges, awkwardness from two people who despise awkwardness.

"Let's take a walk," I say. "It's way too hot in here. When did it get to be so hot?" And Zadie needs to go for a walk anyway, which is just a built-in excuse to keep moving. We need to keep moving.

We walk across Bradford, walk down the steps toward the A-House. Walk through the tight alley past the Julie Heller Gallery, with its big sign—ART. We walk toward my place on the beach. The night is humid, thick, as if the clouds had poured lotion onto it. The dog behaves as if none of our motions are especially unusual, but that's probably her tactic to bring the night back to routine. More than anything Zadie wants routine right now. She must smell the adrenaline, the panoply of human hormone coming off us.

But we don't finish the sentence, because we don't know how to find our way through its logic. Whenever we've tried to imagine through to the end, we've disrupted it, defused it, laughed it off. A sentimental education went into that. The work of years.

So maybe it's easier just to void a pact than it is to say there was something here to lose, right? There's nothing here. There was nothing ever here. Null set, zero.

I can't negotiate from this position, can't agree that we didn't happen, never mattered. Didn't sit and sleep together in a room, not just last night, but the past 365.

Until now, I didn't know there was no point to us, to me.

Canceling time? I will not stand by the idea, no. Je refuse.

Up ahead the spotlight shines from the beam above 411's ground floor. Its joke of light barely illuminates the dune grass, the stand of ragged yuccas along the beach.

I say, "I'm going to stay in my place."

"Come on," Noah says.

I tell him I'm staying in my own bed tonight. I repeat it, as if I'm saying it for someone in the future, who isn't in front of me. Someone I don't know yet. "And you know what? That's it. *This.*"

"*Paul.*"

I can't get the words out without sounding dramatic, and I know Noah is repulsed by my screwed-up expression, the lack of control. But to stay back at the guesthouse tonight? No way. If he wants control, he'll get only half the plate.

Someone else would grab my arm, wrench it behind my back until I punched him, against a bone that wouldn't hurt. We'd talk into the matter until our thoughts calmed. Until we were able to claim ourselves, together and alone again.

We might have made jokes as we strolled back home.

We might have even had sex, hurried sex, along the way. Rough.

But even from the look on his face I can tell he wasn't planning to go here—the night took him out. Probably he expected to have just another Tuesday, and he opened his eye, the wind blew, and a speck of beach got in. And that doesn't mean I forgive.

How long do I cry? Hours? The weekend? The sobbing feels medicinal, as if it's cleansing away possible emergency. I am sobbing for an idea—and I don't even want to know why. But my body seems to require it, this drowning, a bath of warm, salty fluid. The tears stinging my face, my cuff rubbing my cheek over and over until it's skinned, chafed.

My lungs are lakes. I am moving through clear fluid—one of my mother's babies. Parchment? The vanishing twin?

One of us was supposed to die first—one of us was supposed to die.

Sink to the bottom, see?

"Hold them while you can," Mark says.

And I don't know how to deal with the fact that we're both probably going to live.

Sweethearts

"Hi, Mom."

"Hi, Paul."

"You OK, Mom?"

"What's the matter, sweetheart? Your voice sounds funny. You sound like you have a bad cold. You're not getting a head cold now, are you?"

"I'm not sure, I— Well— I just wanted to hear how you were doing."

"I'm doing fine, honey. You're my sweetheart. You know that, Paul, don't you? You're always my sweetheart."

Inappropriate

Out at Longnook Beach, Polly doesn't talk about Noah, or say anything about me. She knows what it is like to be a public couple in

Town, to break up, and to deal with the stresses of people taking one side or the other. People saying the inappropriate, as if a bald criticism of the ex would be a comfort. She knows what I'm in for: people using my breakup as a way to bond with me, or as a way to deal with feeling enraged with their own lovers and partners and that might be why she takes me to the beach, barely a seam between water and sky. A fishing boat out there, and perhaps seals, sea turtles as large as Volkswagen Beetles—invisible beneath the surface. The people on the beach lie out on hot sand as if they're trying to cook the thinking out of themselves.

Sorry

Billy rushes through the door of Waves, where I'm sitting in the hard seats, waiting to get my hair cut. It seems a little strange to be sleeping on my own again these days, which might be why it seems very important to get a haircut, to keep the floors swept, to floss my teeth all the way down, inside the gum line. Billy tacks up an AIDS Support Group Auction flyer to the board. Glances on the way out, stops, then stops again just as he reaches for the door. An old emotion holds him in place.

"I'm sorry," he says, slowing down to look at me with that face he gets when he wants me to see him. It's like he's reached down into the hidden part of him and pulled up the kindly parent. And I don't even know he's there. He's always been there.

The corner of my mouth feels heavy, a little numb. What am I giving off?

Then I think, Yom Kippur? (But he's not Jewish.) Then, Step Nine?

"It was a bad time for me, crazy, complicated. It had nothing to do with you. You know that, right?"

Chemical smell so strong that Jimmy, my haircutter, has to apologize for using it on the woman in the chair. Hair-straightening product that manages to wend its way through my nerves. Billy is still thinking about the two of us, but as for me? Those days are as far away as childhood now.

I thought he just wanted to hunt me, and once he saw he could have me, and more, he lost interest.

"It's OK," I say, just because I'm embarrassed, and I don't know what else.

"That's good," Billy says. "You doing OK? You're looking good. We'll get coffee, catch up sometime." Then he is out the door before I have the chance to answer.

Billy will die of AIDS-related complications in December 1995, my father's birthday.

Caricatures

Above the booths of the Mayflower is a hall of fame, silhouettes of Portuguese locals, both men and women, in caricature. They are both mocking and affectionate, sloped foreheads, big chins and no chins, clown eyes. Not a single face is familiar to me, which means that they're a hall of the dead, dressed up to look like jokers. They have been up so long that the brown paper they're on has been water stained. If anyone took them out of their frames and touched them, that paper would darken and deteriorate, absorbing the oil from their fingers. So they leave them in place.

Noah and I have agreed to meet here, a week after our split. It's no longer the edge of summer, but near Memorial Day. Visitors shifting in their seats: anxious, bored, starving, joyous, electric, mean. We sit near the door, when we should have sat all the way in the back, hidden. If we were in Manhattan, no one would see us or care. But here, in the place of theater, hungry for drama, every gesture is scrutinized, held in, and passed on.

Everyone is too hungry in this town.

What do we talk about? I do most of the talking, and what do I say? Mostly it is pure sound, the sound of: You broke my heart, and I loved you, and you will hear me out. The ancient complaint in its various translations, Job and Jesus and Emma Bovary: Why have you abandoned me? Noah listens with his head down, not talking back. Every so often my eyes wander up to the caricatures because it's hard to look at his face, hard to make him feel so bad. Hard to see *my* face reflected back in his, because feeling must make me look like one of those dead people up on the wall.

Enough

The prospect of open hours makes me anxious, which is why when I get the occasional free afternoon, I bike out to the far west end of Herring Cove. Guys hook up out there, sometimes down a hairpin creek, but more often in the matted impressions in the high dunes, inside a hem of grass, overlooking the sea. It's always late afternoon, too late for the rangers, with their tickets. I have sex with anyone who seems interested in having sex with me. I've decided that there's no point in being picky—maybe there's something to learn from letting go of my idea of a *type*, and what I learn is obvious: that the men out there are probably sweeter than they know to themselves. One evening I have sex with an ottery middle-aged couple just as the sun is going down. They've let themselves go, as it is said when once-attractive people have stopped going to the gym, but they're probably sexier for having given in. Afterward, we lie down, knocking the mosquitoes off each other. I fall asleep on their army blanket, a little crushed between them, as if I am their favorite pup.

Occasionally Noah bikes through Town when I'm outside the store on a break. He says hello, his grin as wide as his face, and doesn't stop. It demolishes me, this biking away from me. *One minute*—he can't check in for a minute? A mutual friend reports his explanation: "I can't talk to Paul now. I need some time." But I decide that that's just a way for him to sound virtuous to himself and others.

As if he genuinely misses me.

Really, I think in the voice of Hollis's Lou.

One day I stop my bike at the top of the highest hill outside the house of Stanley Kunitz and Elise Asher, a house once floated across the harbor from Long Point, fully furnished, intact. Stanley once found a wad of cash in that house that he claimed was the stash of a prostitute, which sounds like the subject of a poem tried out in multiple drafts and never finished. I look down toward the bottom of the hill and race down, my torso upright, without even holding on to the handlebars. I don't even know how to ride a bike without holding on, and somehow I roll on out into flat pavement, by the Provincetown Inn, without crashing into a car or stone column. But there's no one around to observe my feat, which makes me wonder whether it even happened, whether it would have been preferable to break my arm or knock in an eyetooth.

Nevertheless, the aversion of disaster feels weirdly significant. I have been protected in a time of little protection.

A few days after my bike ride, my body decides that it has had enough sex, enough people, even sexy couples gone a little soft. It has no hunger anymore. It has had too much. This body at least has limits and it is time to lay it down to rest.

Est-Ce Tout Là

At the DNA gallery, I'm giving a reading from my new novel, a thread that will eventually fall out of the book. The thread involves a young woman who's photographed by an older man, a situation she's agreed to, until the session starts feeling invasive, manipulative—even though it never has anything explicitly to do with sex. I'm not even sure why this story has captured my attention, and it doesn't exactly help that the famous photographer— the photographer who took the Fellows' portrait in the dunes—is in the second row. He's leaning in, his face especially intent, as if he's scanning me for false notes.

In the front sits Nev, a much younger guy I've been dating. Nev, the former model, who walked down the street like a human lion, looking straight ahead with vulnerability and hauteur. Closer to the back sits Noah, whose presence excites and agitates me. There is a subversive thrill in seeing the two of them together in one space, and I only inflame things by dedicating the reading to Nev.

As soon as I say it, I cringe inwardly at the manipulation, though I know to keep it entirely off my face. But everyone who knows me hears it, and it possibly swallows up their ability to listen to my opening paragraph.

"He never dedicated anything to me," Noah says afterward, in my presence, to a mutual friend. We are in the back of the gallery near the wine, the seltzer, the grapes, the tiny blocks of cheese with their fringed toothpicks. His face is partly miffed, partly wry—the visual equivalent of: est-ce tout là.

I don't deny it and don't try to smooth out the discomfort either. I just let us hang there for a bit. Then he kisses me once on each cheek and walks down the steps.

It doesn't occur to me till much later that he actually might have wanted to hear my work.

Doesn't occur to me till much later that it was probably hell for him to come out tonight. My other friends, the people who once welcomed him, laughed with him, might have been practiced, cool. If they even bothered to look at him as he walked in their direction.

Augustitis

It's deep into summer, the passage in which the locals are porous, cranky, exhausted from working three jobs, tired of demanding tourists who are always, Where's the restroom? Where's the restroom? *Augustitis* is the word commonly used. To be so taxed is to be in an alternate state. It's a bit like abiding the flu, without any of the obvious symptoms. Or like being high when you're not taking hallucinogens. For nearsighted people like me, it's walking through the night without glasses or contact lenses. There's a recognizable shape up ahead—is that Paco? Scott?—with no edges or defining lines. Halos around every light, dense with refracted rainbowy prisms. A hot fog. If everyone's in that state, with none of the usual psychic barriers, anything is possible.

Polly and I bike out to the Love Shack at around 11. There's still plenty of space on the floor, at least forty-five minutes' worth. Then, as if all at once, the crowd grinds human movement to a halt. The air-conditioning all but wheezes out the vent. The smoke is already thick. People who don't usually light up are bumming cigarettes because there's no reason to put up with burning eyes and a scratchy throat without the nicotine. If I could pin a color to the atmosphere, I'd call it turmeric. Polly and I find a corner of the floor where we're free to move, free to locate patterns in the bass we attempt to mimic, echo, physicalize. The point has always been to shut our eyes against sound that is so gorgeous it threatens to damage our eardrums and temporal lobes.

The floor fills up as it always fills up; people beside us dance with drinks in hand, and the loss of space is infuriating. (*Bostonians*!) These are not people who want to dance, who remotely care about it other than to show off, look popular. Too hot, too moist, and we stand off to the side to breathe, to check out whether anyone we like is here.

Who's here? Noah—is that right? Noah, who's been reclusive all summer aside from his late-afternoon trips to the beach. I've never seen him out at night, yet here he is, dancing with a stranger, a guy his height without facial hair, curls on his head, not at all his type. For a time I'm transfixed by the kiss (wonder? shock?), as if I'm watching an animal give birth. It would be one thing if the kissing were just between them, but the kissing is continuous, it's performance, it's ridiculous, a little sad—theater of the ridiculous not just for others, but for me. He must have seen me, he's definitely seen me, and that's all the more reason to demonstrate that he desires and is being desired.

It tears into some membrane of me, the skin between inner and outer. I cannot be reminded of my feelings.

I'm so exhausted I don't even think my knees can hold me up.

"You're an asshole," I yell across frantic, dancing heads. "You're a goddamn fucking asshole, Noah!"

I keep yelling the same thing until I believe he hears me, even though there's no way he could hear above the din. But I could make him see me, all right. And then he does see me: leaping, pointing, aiming my accusatory face in his direction.

And I am the cartoon Tasmanian Devil from the bottom of somebody's fever dream. Not my own dream, because I've never acted like such a total idiot in my life. I've never even called him an asshole, never called any other human close to me an ugly word. My father? Well, that's different. And I'm not even drunk right now, not even close.

Noah walks toward me, but I won't engage as I know it's all too ridiculous. I'm being ridiculous, but that doesn't mean it doesn't hurt, when he stopped feeling any interest in sex.

And yet I put up with that.

Polly leads me out the door, leads me across Shank Painter Road. "Are you all right?" she says, and looks at me as if she doesn't expect an answer. She feels my bewilderment too. She must be thinking of Richard, their breakup, and what led her to stay with me, but she doesn't so much as venture his name.

But something else consumes my grief. What have I done? I've failed my largest assignment: the management of feeling. I've failed at being a man, failed at being a queer man, failed at holding myself together when there are so many actual horrors and tragedies, not just far, but hundreds of feet from us in Town. And I still feel it as failure even when I should be feeling proud for saying, No, don't do that to me, when I know that queer people are always being told, You're shrill, lighten up, get over it, move on, don't take yourself so seriously, look at that little drama queen.

We're the best students of hurting ourselves, and I know that and still manage to use it against myself and others.

Polly and I sit on the step of the broken-down cottage across the street. I've dropped my bike in high weeds and everything around my shoes is glittering, hard: things a crow would notice if it were closer to daylight: cigarette butts, a sheet of chewing gum foil, a fishing hook, an orange peel. I fix my eyes on them because I cannot lift my head. I will not lift my head or say a word because the world cannot be larger than this.

The bass line keeps booming, muffled, from the walls of the club across the street. It's an amplified human heart gone bad, like the two-story heart inside the Franklin Institute of my childhood, so vast and revolting you could take a walk through it.

34

Sixty Days

When it comes to being sick, I'm a professional dating back to childhood. So many speculations about diseases—leukemia, cystic fibrosis—that the speculations, and the dread surrounding them, became sicknesses in themselves. The surrender not just to my body but to the gravity of others surrounding it. My mother's anxiety, her legends: the people around her never stuck around. Even my pediatrician, Doctor Boguslaw, lost his own daughter. Every time a mysterious symptom presented itself in me, he must have been thinking of Nancy, and communicated that to my mother, even if it was just through the set of his mouth, a glance. His worried glance, kind. Doctor Boguslaw.

The bedroom of my childhood. The heat—dry, papery tongue. Too dark in the room to see—what time? My mother sitting on the edge of the bed, leaning over me: "The doctor's going to test your wee-wee." That isn't even her expression; she's always hated childish words for bodily functions, and now she is making a fool of herself, her fear so acute it's consuming her actual language. I see just what they want of me: trapdoor opening in the ceiling, beige, blocky machine lowering upon my midsection. A lens and—an attachment? A crenulated hose from the vacuum cleaner at the car wash. The machine will embarrass me, the machine will poke inside me, hurt me in order to come up with some answer about whether I have to live or die—and the bad news of it will make my mother cry. When I find out I only have to pee into the Dixie cup she holds out for me, I'm so relieved I practically curl up like a grub.

Now it seems surprising that I survived those sixty days, how they came and went like a dream. My throat hurt, my head hurt, my eye sockets, my uvulas, my joints. High fever that wouldn't break. It was hard to sit up, but it was nothing I couldn't handle. In fact, there were benefits in being the center of attention, center of the house, a humming stove in the bedroom, staying all day in my rabbit-patterned pajamas, no one to scare me, no bigger child to make fun of me, or follow me down the hall asking me a simple question over and over as if the whole point had always been to flatten me.

Are you a child or a monkey?

Are you a child or a monkey?

Once I was sent back to school, they'd forgotten I was ever gone, except when it came time to deliver the books from Scholastic. The covers were yellow, shiny, with Curious George's body on the front. Kind and funny George, interested not in being the boss of anyone but in standing *alongside*: that's what I wanted. I never thought I was a ghost until the day the books were delivered. There I was, at the back of the room without a book, and no one in the room thought to hide that, not even the teacher. Back when I was sick my classmates made get-well cards, thirty-two sheets of construction paper folded in half, sketched with the most livid crayons in the Crayola box. Most looked like they were done by children trying to be childish, children who didn't look like they'd meant it. I looked at every one, every day during those sixty days. I thought about each person, how long they spent on each card, how realistic their drawings looked, and gave each one a grade. Only Andrea Fowler got an A+ for her drawing of a clown holding a clutch of red balloons. The lines were straight; she *meant* them. She *wanted* me to get well; it wasn't just homework. Or drawn by a child who needed to look like a child in order to please adults. "That isn't nice," my mother said with an expression that couldn't mask her smile. I didn't have the language to tell her I needed to make my own school, because the school out there wasn't made for the likes of me.

But Curious George: I knew all about lost puzzle pieces: I was the lost puzzle piece in the room in which everyone seemed to be connected, everyone knew each other's names. The day I returned I was reminded it was better to be sick. The teacher scratching Kevin Navins's face, children hiding behind rubber raincoats in the cloakroom, a red-haired girl named Leslie eating an American cheese sandwich in her pee-swamped tartan skirt. Everyone hungry for a fight, the pressure so strong I couldn't even go to the bathroom. When my mother learned that a full sandwich was too much food for me, she found the smallest bread possible, Pepperidge

Farm party slices. "Look at that little sandwich!" cried some boy across the table. "It's a sandwich for a baby. What else is in that bag? Give it up." It didn't occur to me to say no, refuse, and he hated me even more for my compliance. I reached in and found a Tastykake Krimpet. Short, pale, tasteless, frosted the color of a Band-Aid. Didn't my mother know I hated Krimpets, especially butterscotch Krimpets, which were the color of my sick skin? Why did she put me in this position? I can't—I thought, and practically retched. The Krimpet passed from hand to hand till it wasn't even food anymore. No one would eat it after it had been mocked, scorned, laughed at, touched. Another boy jammed it into the spout of his milk carton with such glee that it felt personal, but I was transfixed, I couldn't look away. The Krimpet was me, my sick body. The Krimpet was the lost puzzle piece. The Krimpet was love and optimism and kindness and delight, and now he was shaking the carton so hard I knew it was going to explode all over the table.

Plague Is Your Sister

> The pairing of sex and death in human life is a pairing of intimacy with betrayal, love with violence, and giving of oneself with the taking of life.
>
> WALT ODETS, *In the Shadow of the Epidemic:*
> *Being HIV-Negative in the Age of AIDS*

She's careening toward me, lurching, if such a small person could be said to lurch. Is she weeping? The two of us are on Commercial Street, somewhere near Town Hall. I've never seen Lynda in such awful shape, and when she puts her arms around me she gives me her full weight, though there isn't so much of her left. I feel love, but it is love in its most broken form. Love not just for me—she barely knows me, really—but love for Town, for the people who are sick, the people who are gone. I don't know enough about heroin to say she might be high, or well past that, for if I did I'm sure I'd pull away, say good-bye with a little fear. She says Mark wouldn't let her into the house, and though she is crying about that, she's crying about herself, too, and the force of that pain has enough velocity to break her bones.

I see her as one would see a painting, surreal. Her body breaking itself open, from the inside out.

God

All the photographs and paintings that attempt to represent Town. The same few sites again and again: the ships of MacMillan Wharf, the Pilgrim Monument rising over the trees. Sure, the light might shift on the harbor from Monday to Tuesday, but it's missing the point to make too much of those subtle changes. Looking at those changes straight on? Imagine trying to look at God, and if you think you can do that, God will find a way to break you.

No wonder I hit a point when my ability to speak runs out. And I'm as breathless as if I've been running around the circumference of the world 365 times.

Thirty-five million dead, 1980 —> 2019.

Project for a Recurring Dream Starring the Dune outside Town

Sand filling up the backyards, sand covering up the houses, the bicycles, the roses, until Town's cut off from the Cape, encased below the surface like a new Pompeii. Then a wind coming from the other direction and sweeping the beautiful thing clean. Like the whistling of an enraged inferno.

2018

Afterlife, Notes

At first I felt shame because I had entered
through the door marked *Your Death*.

FRANK BIDART

"I was going to talk to you about that," Steve, my GP, says when I
tell him I'd like to go on PrEP. I fix my eyes on a single window of
the building across Fourteenth Street in an effort to keep casual,
even though my blood pressure tells me the true story. The reading is high, when I've always been told my blood pressure is low.
In two months, it will be back to low, the next time that cuff con-
stricts my arm.

Steve is giving me the full rundown. I'm listening, but it also
helps to concentrate on the action transpiring inside that apartment
window across the street: the electricity humming the refrigerator,
the modem. The pipes leading to the showerhead. The preoccupied
face of the man in the window.

We talk about possible side effects—bone loss, kidney trouble—
and though I'm concerned about all that, I've already made my decision. I won't be taking this drug for decades, like younger men. I
don't have that much time left, though I'm not planning on going
away anytime soon. There's still enough *young* left in me.

Pre-exposure prophylaxis (or PrEP) is when people at very
high risk for HIV take HIV medicines daily to lower their
chances of getting infected. PrEP can stop HIV from taking
hold and spreading throughout your body. It is highly effective
for preventing HIV if used as prescribed, but it is much less

effective when not taken consistently. Daily PrEP reduces the
risk of getting HIV from sex by more than 90%.

CENTERS FOR DISEASE CONTROL AND PREVENTION WEBSITE

Steve calls in the prescription to Duane Reade, but he tells me not
to take the first pill until my blood test says I'm negative. I've been
tested so many times, since a flare-up of shingles ten years ago, that
I've almost forgotten how to be afraid.

All those years I was afraid, and now I look at the filling syringe
as if it's a dream of blood, an art project fed from my vein.

I take the elevator down to the lobby. Out on West Fourteenth, light
hurts my eyes as if it's shining on snow, even though there's almost
no snow left: only dirty, hard crusts. This is no small thing: I've
made a pact to stay around. I couldn't have done that previously. I
should be eating a magnificent dinner for all the times I've lost my
appetite, out of worry for my health.

How many times did HIV fear masquerade as other fears, fear
of friendships, fear of my family, fear of relationships, fear of fucking up?

I start toward Hudson River Park, where men a few years ahead
of me once wandered the piers, years before they were demolished
to become part of a privately funded park of berms, benches, grass,
trees. It was their wonderland, their dream of night above dark
water. Mouth went to mouth, and strangers, for a little while, became known to one another.

Now money sweeps the park clean, along with any traces of lust
and rebellion.

I don't tear open the bag and stare at the bottle until I'm back in
my apartment. A month's supply: *Your insurance saved you $1,995
dollars.*

The absurdity of that figure. I shove the bottle to the back of the
upper shelf, behind the vitamins and teas, as if that move alone could
keep the drug and its price in correct perspective. I'm truly appalled
by it, in awe. I saw too much of how powerful drugs scoured others
when those drugs were brand-new: AZT, Crixivan.

And now I can't ever quit my job. Or more than ever, I'm held hostage by my prescription plan.

Maybe freedom isn't something I'm ready to contend with yet, even though I've bent my life toward freedom.

Am I a top? Or a bottom who's always pretended to be a top? A top out of a shame so deep I can't even feel it in my seat, the shame I grew up attaching to illness? Am I a passive top, or an active bottom? Am I reluctant to give up the status some confer on a top?

Am I still a bottom if I'm ninety-five percent of the time a top, because that's who the people I hook up with manage to conjure up out of me?

The questions of a twenty-two-year-old in his fifties.

An email comes in from the doctor's office informing me that I can access the results of my physical through an online portal.

Only one result strikes my attention: contact with and (suspected) exposure to HIV.

Cold surges. *I'm positive?* Aren't I at least owed a phone call, as in the olden days? I fix on my jade plant across the room, its fleshy leaves, oblong, stained pink-bronze. I don't move from my sofa for an hour. It can't be. But I don't know that for sure until two days pass, and I get a voicemail from Steve, who ticks off my results, including HIV-negative, from part of a long list of tests.

HIV doesn't even fall at the top anymore.

Contact with and (suspected) exposure to HIV: recommended ICD-10-CM codes.

A whole month passes before I tap the first hard blue capsule onto my palm.

After I swallow there's a surge of vitality—my body certainly registers change. It's like taking an antidepressant for the first time, or a double espresso for the blood cells. I wait for some other reaction—a stomachache, bloatedness, nausea, a tiny needle of a headache? Should I drink extra water? Eat a snack? But nothing.

And on the second day, I register as much difference as I do when

I take a multivitamin. Then my body gets used to it, as the body gets used to almost anything new.

When people in their twenties swallow this pill, they take a different story into their body. And that doesn't mean I feel higher in rank, or resent them for coming into the world at a later time.

But you don't understand, I want to say.

The HR person on the other end of the line sounds casual and almost indifferent when I bring up my concerns about prescription coverage. I'm about to do a visiting semester at a university in Austin and I'm trying not to panic about cost.

"I take a very expensive prescription," I say in a ragged voice, as a way to instill alarm, a wake-up call. I don't say, It is keeping me alive, but I want to because it is.

The HR person is unflappable, not to be drawn into my feelings. I don't understand till much later that my anxiety is also about another matter: I'd forgotten I wasn't positive.

Now that I have freedom, it's more complicated than I'd ever expected it to be. HIV never stopped me from having sex, but now that I can have any kind of sex, I don't know exactly what I want. I sign on to Scruff, look at the faces I've seen a hundred times from Brooklyn. Look at Pornhub, scroll through so many titles I get overwhelmed to the point of distraction and fall asleep with the laptop open on the covers: *Beefy Homo Dog Relaxed with Passionate Toe Sucking*, *Muscle Daddy Gives Proper Breeding*, *Real Straight Dude Made a Gay Porn in Spite of Him*, *Pig Boy Meets His Daddy*, *Lending a Hand and Mouth to a Guy in a Cast*.

Abundance might be an enemy to desire, but that doesn't mean I would want to be back in the 1990s. Nostalgia, especially nostalgia of that kind, is murderous.

Note: AIDS isn't the good old days.

What I could have made out of the fear I held back.

By which I mean: How many brain cells were burned up, extinguished?

His breathing quickens, eyes tighten, I tell him to come into me, "Yes, you can come inside," and he does so with a groan, and we're scorched. I tell him not to move, tell him to stay still, yes, just like that, and we lie quiet, curling into each other, his chest rough and electric against my back. In a little while, I want to pull away, can feel him falling asleep, but then I must too. When my eyes open, an hour's passed. The room in Brooklyn alight like a cabin in the woods, but with the sounds of a dog out on the street, howling in imitation of an ambulance.

These could be golden years, like the first years after Stonewall, when the Village swarmed with vitality, when sex was a Political Act: the making up of a community, encounter by encounter, and no one was (yet) contending with a plague.

But we have other matters to fight for these days.

Linda Villarosa: "In certain pockets of the country, unknown to most Americans, H.I.V. is still ravaging communities at staggering rates." Jackson, Columbia, El Paso, Augusta, Baton Rouge

Danez Smith: "he left me his blood / & though he is not dead / i miss my husband"

A wildly handsome bearded man in his twenties lies on a circular table. The room is almost dark, lit only by a red bare bulb in the ceiling. He doesn't behave like a handsome young man who's learned the power of withholding. He's anything but withholding—sex with four men at once. Every orifice packed and filled. There's no fear in his face or body, no resistance. No hand raised to say pull out when one man's face tightens in ecstasy. No fear about being interpreted as a slut, none of those worn-out cares about self-destruction. He's simply a young man who hasn't had to take the costs of a plague into his blood. He isn't rebelling, isn't saying fuck you to the parents who could have disinherited him, kicked him out of their house, said unforgivable words. He's not hiding. Not envisioning a premature death, not contending with the deaths of ten friends, twenty-five friends, keep going. I'm in awe. When he gets home he'll toss some green vegetables into a clear glass bowl.

Solitude is the scent of the man ahead of me, his hair, his shoulders, his cuffs. That scent involves a combination of cigarette smoke, adrenaline, light sweat on denim, cedar beard oil. I'm sure he thinks he's passing as someone who isn't traumatized, isn't hurt. I'm sure he doesn't think his secret's out, but it's all over him. I sound like I'm talking about someone disheveled, down on his luck, but he's impeccably presented, beard trimmed, his cuffs folded to show off an inch of tangerine sock above his shoe. Even though he's a handsome man, others are giving him a wide berth. They speed up when they catch themselves walking beside him. I can practically sense his antennae—he jumps when a hubcap scrapes against the curb. What terrible thing has happened to him? Which wound tearing into his psyche? It's devouring him, taking him whole, as he attempts and fails to heal it. I watch how he watches—his curiosity suggests he's queer, not accustomed to disappearing into himself. For the briefest instant he makes eye contact with me and turns away, as if his gaze stores voltage. His gaze would be easier to take if I didn't believe he saw the same voltage in me.

"I just want you to know I'm positive and undetectable," texts a man I'm getting to know.

I wait some minutes before I answer. I want to sound casual, but casual in a way that doesn't seem glib, that doesn't make him think he's out of touch. I could remind him that undetectable people can't transmit HIV, and I'm stupefied that he might not be aware of that. That's a burden he doesn't need on top of any others.

How many simply walked away when the word *positive* came up?

"Totally fine," I text. "I'm HIV-negative and on PrEP."

And there's no mistaking his relief, or the gravity implied by it, even though we're not exactly face-to-face. When I go over to his place the next night, we talk for a while on his sofa. Laugh about the holidays and their crazy burdens, laugh about the people who don't tell us when their gifts arrive, and when we move to his bedroom, I watch how he tears open a condom between his teeth. The finesse of it is impressive. He's had plenty of practice.

I tell him, "You know, you don't have to use that. You don't have to put that on."

The frisson of saying those words aloud, asking him to lay it down, be present. Skin to skin. An element of closeness and danger I don't ever take for granted.

But he keeps his head low. Doesn't acknowledge my words. Maybe he's wary of any drug's power, even though they've probably kept him alive for a long time. But I don't know him well enough for such a conversation, not now. What better way to extinguish desire?

He won't admit that the world has changed, is changing. To knock down the tower he's built? That would be like demolishing the Empire State.

He's acting out of care, I remind myself.

"Each tablet contains 200 mg of emtricitabine and 300 mg of tenofovir disoproxil fumarate, which is equivalent to 245 mg of tenofovir disoproxil." Truvada (PrEP)

A grad student of mine tells me about a friend of hers who has an expression for any book written about AIDS: *trauma porn.* Then he checks an incoming message from his phone, leaves half his salad on his plate, and goes out to have sex at one thirty in the afternoon.

"Oh God," I say, then begin to crack up out of shock.

"Exactly!" my student says, laughing along.

When I'm not having enough sex, say, when weeks go by when I haven't made time for sex—there is my father at the back of my imagination, telling me I'm not getting my money's worth.

You're paying for that drug, he insists. Get out there.

Do I have to? I say back.

Then the same father says, Why should I have to pay into a system for people who can't control themselves?

Three years ago I fled from Philadelphia to Town on the day after my father died, because I didn't want to be anywhere else. I bought a plane ticket almost instantly. Distraction, company, familiar jokes, casual acquaintances, animals, laughter—where else could I find that particular combination but Town?

In the wake of death, I went to the place I associate with death.

My Ganges, but a spit of sand rather than a river. And I started to write.

One day later it still feels surreal to put this down. I don't think any other being wanted to live more. In the past six months he lived through two separate bedside vigils, three separate stays in the hospice wing of the hospital, lived through nurses and caretakers who didn't want him to get out of bed when all he wanted was to walk, walk, walk. Just over thirty-six hours ago I was teaching Maggie Nelson's The Argonauts *to a workshop full of writers, and a student asked to read this passage from late in the book: "[Death] will do you even if you don't believe it will do you, and it will do you in its own way. There's never been a human that it didn't." I think a very small part of me might have believed that he was another kind of human. Maybe he'd escape it, find some way to solve it, fix it, which was true to how he approached everything, to-do lists and problems and procedures, ever the engineer—though he just as often put those problems aside to work on the next thing. He never sat still.*

He was ninety-one years old.

In my mind every death will always be an AIDS death; everyone will always die before their time, whether they're twenty-one or ninety-one. Nobody will ever get enough affection; everyone will be abandoned emotionally by the people they'd counted on, who get hardened by procedures, the insurance industry, the medical establishment, the funeral industry at the end. And for all that's against their terrible journey, the dead burn brighter to me than they do when they're alive.

Another trip. A holiday this time, Polly about to go to Kent and I'm watching her dog, Petey, for Thanksgiving week. I walk Petey down Commercial, toward Montello Street, and Town is quieter than I expected it to be. I'm in one of those moods when I'm not thinking that the Town I remember is gone. I'm not thinking what I too often find myself brooding about these days: too rich, too white, platform for Airbnbs, flipping, gentrification, everyone over fifty-five. Where's my little city of the young? Instead, my body reminds me how safe I feel, how well I slept through last night, all night. Safety different from the safety of 1991, but safety nonetheless. Petey feels it too. And that awareness pulses back and forth through the leash, which goes slack only when he sniffs and licks a plant leaf. Petey, who thinks of me as his father, or his best friend. Human boyfriend? It's impossible not to wonder that when he's lying on his side, looking up at me from his corduroy bed, which takes up a sizable portion of the small living room. He's communicating a contract through brown eyes: You're mine.

Mine.

Then he's dashed out of his leash, or broken his leash—or what? Slipped out of his collar. Time slows, and all sound rushes out of the world. Petey dashes toward the two Akitas on the street. Does Petey bite, or just threaten to, and what's he trying to protect? Barks tear the air, but the Akitas look all right, Petey looks all right, no blood on any coat, the humans jerk their dogs apart, but the humans are not OK, not OK at all. The Akitas' human is wailing. Her safe space's been violated, and that's the last thing she must have expected on a sunny, frigid day. Petey's robbed her of her Town. And me? I'm immobilized, as if I've stepped on an electric wire. I'm kneeling, curling my body around Petey to keep him close against the sound of her pain, which whips like a belt on the ground. His heart beats into my palm, his face stunned, ashamed, the domestic side hunted by his wild, which usually feels distant unless he's running through the woods, crashing through briars. He's so used to being good, labeled the dear, smart, loyal boy by his humans, and now he's slipped out of his category. I hold him so close he looks confused by me. I say, "I'm sorry" to her, "very sorry," but it's not enough, and never will be. And all the bodies that were lost in Town, smell of sickness on fingers, ambulance pulling up, silent, in the middle of the night, very sorry—and Petey's one of those bodies. Could I even begin to communicate that to a stranger? Could a late arrival to Town ever understand? "You know what?" she says. "I'm calling the police." The police? You can't do that, I want to say. Holy ground. I'm still holding on to Petey and the world outside of Town pours into Town. Town replenishes itself and we won't ever get it back. Once we would have worked this out on our own, would have laughed after tense words, would have offered to take each other out for a coffee, but it's 2018, and the world's too hurt for kindnesses like that. The hour's too late. And though the police will eventually show up, in extraordinary calm with a suggestion for a harness, and a sturdy one at that, the terms of Town have changed. Two narratives of damage collide—where does *her* story begin? And now the two of us must write new narratives—bolder, more outlandish, unresolved—or our safe Town will be gone for good.

If you really love a place, you'll be able to walk with its flaws. Not to love the flaws, not to accept them. Hell, you might even hate the flaws, no reason to describe a world in which hate wasn't ever ground together with love. Thus, you'll be able to say Town is about as hard to get to as Tierra del Fuego, and if you should need to leave in a hurry, know the sky will darken, a storm will blow up, all modes of transportation will be canceled, and the wind will blow and blow for the next twenty-five years. You'll be able to admit that Commercial Street in summer isn't the charming narrow lane it appears to be, but a ruthless chute in which you're a candlepin against a rolled bowling ball: one-way car traffic against two-way bike traffic, delivery trucks, the widest SUVs, widest strollers on the market, skateboards, the Town trolley, pickup trucks with extended rearview mirrors, motorcycles, fire trucks, runners, bachelorettes, three muscle bears in an oncoming row, seniors fresh off the cruise ship, aggressive walkers, texting walkers, brain-freeze walkers, ferry travelers with roller bags, occasional clueless straight couples who hold on to each other's hands for dear life, no idea what they've gotten themselves into. You'll say that certain locales occasionally smell of a most distinctive conflation of elements: low tide, decaying plant matter, fried clam, semen on wet sand, fox pee, beer on breath, salt air, weed. You'll say it's the kind of place where the first person you're likely to run into is the last person you'd ever want to see—say the guy who still holds a grudge against you for pushing him away at the Boatyard in 1993.

And sometimes when I'm touched I think, I am in life—and that's an entirely new sensation. I'm not standing apart from myself, watching myself. To think that I've lived long enough to live through fear.

But Jackson, Columbia, El Paso, Augusta, Baton Rouge. In some parts of the world HIV is only beginning.

Tender boat, still afloat, even though it's springing leaks, one in the front, one in the back. As easy to tear open as skin. It was always meant to be a wreck, wasn't it? If I try to fill it with gifts for the dead, will it make it over that wave ahead, or will it sink right to the bottom, become a cavern for fish?

And what better place to go back to than my first full night in Town? And here I could talk about the kindness that met me when I went into the Work Center office to pick up my instructions and key. And here I could say I didn't even mind how many times I banged my head against the low ceiling of my room. Seven months ahead of time, pure time. I could shoot a tiny movie right here, a movie that stands for hope, the end of isolation and the promise of company in a brute age. Is it possible to write joy? If I could write joy it would be like soldering five sentences on top of one another. It would be the smell of heart tissue in attack mode, or the dread that comes with any beginning, the body knowledge that the new is its own kind of death. And maybe that's why I need to keep moving after taking every last thing out of my cherry-red hatchback.

I want to touch you while there's still time to touch you.

Permission acknowledgments

Acknowledgments

I'd like to thank the Corporation of Yaddo, the John Simon Guggenheim Memorial Foundation, the Returning Residency Program of the Fine Arts Work Center in Provincetown, and Rutgers University for vital support that helped this book come into being.

And deepest thanks to:

Matt McGowan — Michael Taeckens — Fiona McCrae — Steve Woodward — the rest of the editorial team at Graywolf, including Katie Dublinski, Jeff Shotts, Ethan Nosowsky, Chantz Erolin, Susannah Sharpless, and Yana Makuwa — the marketing team at Graywolf, including Marisa Atkinson, Morgan LaRocca, Casey O'Neil, Caroline Nitz, Karen Gu, and Mattan Comay — Leslie Johnson and Josh Ostergaard — Ill Nippashi-Hoereth — Beowulf Sheehan — Kapo Ng — Polly Burnell — Elizabeth McCracken, Edward Carey, Gus Harvey, and Matilda Harvey — Petey — Anna deVries — Mark Doty — Ned — Dawn Walsh — Danella Carter — Richard Baker — Daphne Klein — Eloise Morley — my colleagues and students in the MFA Program at Rutgers University–Camden, including Lisa Zeidner, Lauren Grodstein, Greg Pardlo, and Pat Rosal — Stephanie Manuzak — Deb Olin Unferth — Leah Dawson — Chris Busa, Susanna Ralli, Irene Lipton, Ingrid Aue, and Annie Sloniker at *Provincetown Arts* — Matt Klam, Claire Vaye Watkins, Lisa Olstein, Carl Phillips, Garth Greenwell, and Victoria Redel — Brenda Shaughnessy — Dara Wier — Joy Williams — the Fine Arts Work Center — the community of Provincetown, Massachusetts: everyone who lived and died.

PAUL LISICKY is the author of *Lawnboy, Famous Builder, The Burning House, Unbuilt Projects,* and *The Narrow Door: A Memoir of Friendship.* His work has appeared in the *Atlantic, BuzzFeed, Conjunctions, Fence, Foglifter,* the *New York Times Book Review,* and the *Offing,* among other magazines and anthologies. He is a graduate of the Iowa Writers' Workshop, and his awards include fellowships from the Guggenheim Foundation, the National Endowment for the Arts, and the Fine Arts Work Center in Provincetown, where he has served on the Writing Committee since 2000. He has taught in the creative writing programs at Cornell University, New York University, Sarah Lawrence College, the University of Texas at Austin, and elsewhere. He is currently an associate professor in the MFA Program at Rutgers University–Camden, where he is the editor of *StoryQuarterly.* He lives in Brooklyn.

The text of *Later* is set in Sabon LT Pro.
Book design by Ann Sudmeier. Composition by
Bookmobile Design & Digital Publisher Services,
Minneapolis, Minnesota. Manufactured by McNaughton & Gunn
on acid-free, 30 percent postconsumer wastepaper.